# *Historic* —— MOVIE THEATERS *of* COLUMBIA MISSOURI

# *Historic* MOVIE THEATERS *of* COLUMBIA MISSOURI

DIANNA BORSI O'BRIEN

THE
History
PRESS

Published by The History Press
Charleston, SC
www.historypress.com

*Front cover, top, left to right*: This 1965 Missouri Theatre concession stand was installed by Commonwealth, reputed to be the first concession stand in the theater. *Collection of S Barre Barrett*; the Parkade Drive-In Theatre opened in 1953 where Parkade Plaza is today. *Collection of Judy Jeans Glaister*; Frank and Anna Barrett, Rex P. Barrett's parents, in the Uptown concession shop, before it was inside the theater. *Collection of S Barre Barrett*; *bottom*: The Uptown Theatre. *Collection of S Barre Barrett*.
*Back cover*: Columbia Theatre, 1907. *Collections of the Boone County Historical Society*.

First published 2021

Manufactured in the United States

ISBN 9781467146401

Library of Congress Control Number: 2021943561

*Notice*: The information in this book is true and complete to the best of our knowledge. It is offered without guarantee on the part of the author or The History Press. The author and The History Press disclaim all liability in connection with the use of this book.

# CONTENTS

# CONTENTS

# ACKNOWLEDGEMENTS

This book is the work of dozens of people who gave me their time, support and information to help me piece together the history of Columbia's movie theaters, many of them almost lost in the mists of history.

But the person I owe the greatest thanks to is my husband, David. Without his steadfast love and patience—and his willingness to read and correct every single draft of this book—I'd still be back on page 1.

We all need to thank Joe Arpad, a historian and old friend, for his suggestion to make this a book not just about movie houses but about the people who built, operated and loved them.

A big shout out to Amanda J. Staley Harrison for her extreme patience! Two years ago, Amanda, a member of the Mayor's Task Force for Columbia's Bicentennial Celebration, asked me if I could put together a timeline of Columbia's theaters. I said sure, and well, it didn't happen as fast as I had hoped, but here it is. Along the way, I've really appreciated the support and the laughter we shared at lunch.

This book would not have been possible without everyone who was willing to answer a telephone call, Facebook message, email or text from someone they didn't know. I appreciate their willingness to answer my endless questions, tell me stories about themselves or their families in the movie theater business and look for photographs, scrapbooks and mementos buried in their basements and attics. Thanks to Mary Beth Brown, Cullen Cline, Ashley Davis, Patrick Earney, Jim Ewing, Matt Gerding, Lawrence

Lile, Marty Loring, Richard King, Melina Loggia, Tom Mendenhall, Don Mueller, Monica Senecal Palmer, Gina Rende, Debbie Richerson, Tom R. Shrout Jr., Dennis Stork, Ed Tibbs, Lili Vianello, Lucy Vianello, Robert Wells, Jeff Westbrook, James Whitt and Sehon Williams.

A special thanks to Michael Cochran, Christine King and Mark Neenan, who brought to light the forgotten history of the Varsity as a furniture store and a cheese shop.

Also thanks to Mary Palmer for reminding me about the lighter side of movie theaters. I also appreciated the time Judy Jeans Glaister spent with me explaining that growing up literally in the drive-in wasn't all fun and games. Also, thanks to Jami Durham of the Galveston Historical Foundation for making getting priceless images from Judy possible.

I'm especially grateful to S Barre Barrett, who shared his family history with me and spent time telling me about his amazing father, Rex P. Barrett, as well as the rest of his family. Barre went the extra mile by lending me priceless family artifacts and documents as well. I also appreciate his patience and that of his nephew Ted Pettit in helping me understand the new business model Commonwealth Theaters brought to town.

I wish I could thank Harold Nichols, but unfortunately he died before this book was published. His enthusiasm in talking about the movie theaters of the 1940s and 1950s opened a door to the past for me from a time when a kid could go from popcorn boy to projectionist and experience the thrill of keeping up with the weekly adventures of Boston Blackie and Flash Gordon. His enthusiasm and kindness will stay with me forever.

I want to thank Barbra Horrell for her time and patience helping me understand the influence and layers of racism and its continuing effects in our lives.

Kudos to David Wilson of Ragtag, who carved out time to talk to me right before it put on the first ever outdoor True/False Film Fest at Stephens Park amid the coronavirus limitations. Also deep appreciation to Paul Sturtz, who also took time out to recall the early days of Ragtag while starting a new job as the co-director of Upstate Films in Rhinebeck, New York.

A big thank-you to Ashley Brown of Lindner Properties, who went the extra mile to make sure I got the only image I've ever seen of the original Forum Theatre. Thanks to Garry Lewis for meeting with me to share his story of saving the Hall and the Varsity. I appreciate Sheri Biehl Casady's insight into the Hall's time as a jewelry store.

The stories people told me provided depth, but research provided the backbone of this book.

Many of the details of the lives of the people who built the movie theaters would have been lost without the work of Nancy Obermiller Kiser and her magical way of finding online information on newspapers.com and ancestry.com. Her work helped bring people to life.

Deep thanks to Chris Campbell of the Boone County History & Culture Center and Carolyn Collings and Nancy Thomas at the center's research library for their amazingly kind patience and searching for artifacts, images and the citations to go with them.

I appreciate the help of Sandy Schiefer, archivist at the *Columbia Missourian* and librarian at the Missouri School of Journalism, for copies of hard-to-find newspaper articles, which saved me countless hours of staring at microfilm.

There are not enough thank-yous in the world to express my appreciation to the entire staff at the State Historic Society of Missouri Research Center–Columbia, from gently showing me how to work the microfilm machine more than once to letting me into the microfilm room even when I didn't make an appointment (which I pretty much never did). The whole staff is magical, finding resources I would never have found without them.

Our local Columbia Public Library is an invaluable resource, from providing online access to the yearbooks of Columbia's high schools to the onsite resources, including city directories and the almost unknown but massively helpful vertical files to finding me a last-minute citation of a rare book.

Words fail me for how much I appreciate two people who did more than help me when it came to the images for this book. First, there are not enough words to say thank you to Deanna Dikeman, who crawled through a little hole in the wall in the Hall Theatre to get images on a hot day and took the amazing images of six of the theaters all at the last minute. Then there is Ginny Booker, who deserves a special place in heaven for agreeing to help me manage all these images and more importantly for being a friend I can laugh with when I'm panicking.

A special thanks to Laura Jolley, assistant director of manuscripts at the Center for Missouri Studies at the State Historic Society of Missouri, for going back to search over and over for images as I kept coming up with one more photo I just had to have…and for getting them all scanned so quickly.

Thank you to Greg Olson, a real historian, who never once seemed to think it was odd that a journalist was attempting to write a book about the history of movie theaters and encouraged me along the way. And thanks to Columbia mayor Brian Treece, who always bolstered my confidence when we'd see each other and said how much he was looking forward to reading my book.

As for confidence, thanks to Carolyn Paris, my life coach, who helped me remember that there is power in asking for help. I want to say a special thank-you to accountability buddy and friend Christine Weddle. Finally, last but certainly not least, thanks to all my friends and family members who laughed with me, let me cry along the way and always reminded me that I'm never alone and you can do anything—even write a book about Columbia's movie theaters—one day at a time.

# PART I

# MOVIES COME TO COLUMBIA

# 1

# WHY MOVIE THEATERS MATTER

Everyone has a story to tell about going to the movie theater, whether it's where they had their first date, their first kiss, their first job or simply enjoyed family outings. Movie theaters are a part of everyone's lives. Even if we can stream a movie, there's something special about going to a movie theater and sharing that experience that gives us a sense of belonging and community.

Everyone also has a favorite movie theater or interest in a movie theater, so this book is organized by the individual theater in order of its opening date. Each chapter of this book covers a specific Columbia movie theater from its opening to the present or until it closed—all twenty-eight of them.

The first movie was shown in Columbia in 1897, and since then, the city and the country have undergone tremendous changes in the economy, technology, race relations, class, gender roles and sexual mores. Movie theaters are important because all of these changes have been reflected in the kinds of theaters we have, where they are and what they show.

In the more than one hundred years since the first movies were shown, they've grown from a novelty shown periodically advertised by handbills in the early 1900s, to the movie palaces of the 1920s of more than one thousand seats each flooded with crowds of people who went to the movies two or three times a week, to a staple of entertainment. Movie theaters changed, too, from converted dramatic theaters and storefronts to movie palaces to purpose-built box-like auditoriums.

The 1920–30 golden era of movie theaters faded after television arrived in 1948, but Columbia remained a movie theater kind of town throughout the decades. Despite challenges and closures of the 2020–21 pandemic, Columbia's two suburban multiplexes, the Forum 8 and the Regal Columbia RPX, the Olde Un Theatres and the independent two-screen Ragtag Cinema have survived.

The 2020–21 coronavirus took its toll. All the movie theaters closed in March 2020, but the Forum 8 and the Ragtag quickly reopened. The fourteen-screen Regal, the former Hollywood Stadium 14, stayed closed from October 2020 until May 2021. And despite pandemic-related restrictions, the Ragtag Film Society put on its annual international documentary True/False Film Fest, a bit later than its usual February time slot, and the 2021 fest was held outside in Stephens Park from May 5 to 8, 2021.

The start of Columbia's movie theater industry was not dramatic. In 1897, when the first photoplay exhibitions were shown, they attracted little attention. The first movies were shown at the Haden Opera House as a novelty entertainment. Over the next few years, saloons, hat stores, warehouses and even churches would be used to show movies, which were called photoplays, picture exhibitions and motion pictures. Those first moving images were shocking at first, not because of the content but because seeing an image move was something entirely new.

In fact, at first the content of the movies was mundane and the movies were short, sometimes just a minute, with no storyline or plot. Early movies showed common things like a wave hitting the shore, a train arriving at a station or people leaving work. These images were so surprising that there are reports that people cowered when they saw the wave coming in toward them.

## WHEN MOVIES ARRIVED

In 1897, people were yearning for entertainment. Before movies arrived, the only theatrical entertainment available was concerts or plays—if a person could afford it. The first movies cost a nickel, but a play or concert could command as much as $1.50 per person.

As a result, for most people entertainment meant church socials and traveling acts such as vaudeville, circuses or Wild West shows. For men, there were saloons and billiard halls. Family entertainment included county fairs, parades, horse races and later bicycling and roller skating, which became popular after the Civil War. Other popular options were speeches and lectures by local or national luminaries. Politicians drew huge crowds. In 1896, 1906 and 1918, people flocked to hear three-time presidential candidate William Jennings Bryan.[1]

Going anywhere when movies first arrived wasn't easy. There were no cars. Broadway wasn't paved until 1906. The privately owned Columbia Water and Light Company was established in 1893, but the city's waterworks and electric plant wouldn't open until 1904. Without lighting, people, especially women, didn't feel safe out in the evenings.

Then, as people moved from farms to the city to work in Columbia's growing retail, education, healthcare and light manufacturing sectors, this change led to an increase in the available leisure time and the demand for entertainment grew. As movie technology developed, Columbia's theater industry and population grew right along with it.

From 1890 to 1900, the city's population grew 41 percent to 5,651 from 4,000 people. The city had one movie venue, the Haden Opera House, and movies were also shown in churches. At first, movies were just fillers, something to show between vaudeville acts that might include singing, dancing, juggling and even dog tricks. At other times, movies were used as "chasers"—something to get people to empty their seats after a vaudeville show so the next audience could take their place.

But within a few years, moving pictures began to tell stories, and people began showing up in droves. Columbia was growing as well. From 1900 to 1910, the city's population increased by 71 percent, and by 1909, Columbia had seven movie theaters, including the Airdome, which could seat two thousand—in a town of less than ten thousand.

Racism also showed up at the movie theaters. The 1894 Haden Opera House was segregated, as were all the movie theaters until the 1950s–60s. The Missouri Theatre forced Black patrons to use a side door and climb steep stairs to the balcony. Some movie theaters, including the Nickelodeon, barred Black people from admittance entirely. In 1909, three University of Missouri students opened Negro Nickelodeon to give "them" a place of their own to go, as a newspaper stated it at the time.

World War I slowed the city's population growth, but it rebounded from 1920 to 1930 and the city grew by 44 percent. From 1916 to 1928, Columbia gained three massive movie houses: the Hall, Varsity and Missouri.

In the 1930s, radio began to make inroads, and nationally movie theater owners were complaining that the weekly movie attendance rate had fallen to 65 percent. By contrast, in 2000, only 10 percent of people went to the movies once a week.

In 1948, movie theaters' largest competitor—television—got a boost from an antitrust Supreme Court ruling that said movie studios were operating a monopoly by producing, distributing and showing the movies in their own theaters. At that time, theaters were forced to either buy a studio's entire output of movies or none, sight unseen. Columbia never had a movie studio–owned theater, but most cities did. The Fox Theatre in St. Louis, for example, opened in 1929 as part of William Fox's motion picture organization.

When movie studio owners realized the 1948 ruling might force them to sell off their movie theaters and lose that income flow, they began to sell their back library of movies to television stations, giving television a boost.[2]

In 1948, there were 108 television stations in the United States, up from 3 in 1941. Columbia's first television station, NBC affiliate KOMU, opened on December 21, 1953. It remains the nation's only commercial major-network affiliate television station where students work in its newsroom as a working laboratory.

TV ownership matched the growth of television stations. In 1950, only 9 percent of households had a television set; by 1955, that number hit two-thirds of households. Ten years later, televisions were in 90 percent of homes, and by 2011, the number was 96.7 percent.

## DRIVE-IN MANIA

Following World War II, former soldiers flocked to Columbia to use their GI benefits, and the city's population grew by 74 percent. But movie theaters faced three new challenges: the move to the suburbs, the shift to automobile transportation and the inroads of television. As a result, Columbia's theaters, all concentrated downtown, saw a downturn in attendance. The city's movie theater owners responded by building three drive-in theaters.

The next population surge was from 1960 to 1970, when Columbia saw a 60 percent increase and the population hit 58,512. As cars became the primary mode of transportation, movie theaters opened in suburban shopping centers.

The city's population growth slowed during the 1980s and 1990s, when the city grew only 6 percent and 11 percent, respectively. From 1990 to 2000, Columbia saw a 22 percent increase, and the city grew more than 25 percent when the population hit 108,500 in 2010.

As the suburbs continued to grow and shopping centers began to develop, a new trend was toward building multiplex movie theaters surrounded by a parking lot. But in 1998, two young men grew hungry for movies beyond mainstream moneymakers, and Ragtag Cinema got its start as a series of movies shown at The Blue Note, a 1927 theater. Ragtag would later move into a spot on Tenth Street before moving to its current space in a rehabbed Coca-Cola bottling plant on Hitt Street.

Since that first photo exhibition at the Haden Opera House at Broadway and Ninth, movies have become part of our lives in Columbia. As of 2021, the movie industry is a $100 billion market and we can watch movies on our smartphones, televisions or even our watches, yet we still go to movie theaters. Why? My nineteen-year-old granddaughter, who grew up with movies on demand, said it best: "I always enjoy going for the food and the experience of going to a movie."

She knows—there's just something about going to the movies.

# PART II

# IS IT AN OPERA HOUSE OR A SALOON?

# 2

# THE HADEN OPERA HOUSE, 1894–1901

## COLUMBIA'S FIRST MOVIE THEATER

The Haden Opera House was the venue for the first movie shown in Columbia as noted in 1897. The first theater built for movies wouldn't come along until 1909.

In 1901, the opulent three-story stone building at Broadway and Ninth Streets burned to the ground in a blaze called one of Columbia's worst. No one was injured in the fire, but the loss was estimated at $60,000, or what would be $1.9 million in 2021 dollars.

Later, two more buildings at the northeast corner on Broadway, the 2021 location of Commerce Bank, burned as well. The Haden Opera House fire was blamed on an overheated furnace and fueled by the "huge store of coal in the basement."[3]

After the fire, Columbia was without a movie venue for at least a year and perhaps longer. Reports about when the next movie venue, the Airdome, opened conflict; coincidentally, it was opened by B.E. Hatton, the manager of the Haden when it burned.

The name Haden House came up again from 1975 to 1982 as an upscale restaurant at 4515 Highway 763 North in the former home of Joel H. Haden, who built the Haden Opera House. That building replaced an earlier Haden home that had burned down between 1898 and 1905.[4]

## MAKING HISTORY

The Haden Opera House, sometimes spelled Hayden, saw Columbia's "largest and most cultured and fashionable audience ever assembled."[5]

The Haden Opera House, circa 1895. From the book *Columbia Missouri Herald 25th Anniversary 1870–1895. Collections of the Boone County Historical Society.*

It opened with a performance of the Madison Square Theatrical Troupe of New York.

The Haden featured 1,246 seats and four curtained and upholstered private boxes. The *Weekly Missouri Statesman* noted that "colored people" had to sit in a balcony above the first balcony. Such segregation was legal due to the 1896 U.S. Supreme Court *Plessy vs. Ferguson* ruling that ruled separate facilities were constitutional.

The opera house occupied the second and third floor of the building while the street level was occupied by retail, including the W.B. Nowell Grocery Co. and the N.D. Evans drugstore.[6]

## NO FANFARE

As noted, the first movies drew little attention. The only notice was in the May 28, 1897 newspaper, which stated: "The Vitascope exhibitions at Haden Opera House this week have proven of unusual interest and attractiveness. The graphophone was employed between acts while the pictures shown were presented in fine style."[7]

The Haden Opera House, 1901. *Collections of the State Historical Society of Missouri.*

While this was the first documented movie in Columbia, it is likely there were previous exhibits.[8] Previous movies were probably advertised by handbills rather than with a newspaper ad.

A Vitascope was one of the earliest movie projectors, and the "moving pictures" or "photo plays" could be shown on a canvas hung on the wall or on the wall itself. At that time, all movies would have been shown on equipment brought to town by a traveling company, which would have been either a Vitascope or a Kinetoscope.

While Vitascope could show images to an audience, a Kinetoscope showed the images on a single-viewer cabinet—these were sometimes called peep shows. The Kinetoscope was quickly abandoned as early entrepreneurs learned they could make more money showing a photo exhibition to a crowd rather than to one person at a time.

# THE AIRDOME, 1902–1919

## FROM TENT THEATER TO SKATING RINK

Columbia's second movie venue, the Airdome theater, was primitive, with no roof and a board fence, according to a 1908 Sanborn fire insurance map that showed it between Sixth and Seventh Streets on Broadway. Sanborn maps include descriptions of building materials, such as whether the building is brick or wood, and other details as related to the potential for a fire.

Hatton, the former manager of the Haden, later claimed he opened the Airdome in 1902, making it the state's second "airdome," or outdoor movie theater, and at that time it was south of the Wabash station at Walnut and Tenth Streets.[9] There are no historic documents confirming that date or location.

By 1909, ads state the Airdome was at Tenth and Walnut, where in 1918 it became a roller rink before burning on February 18, 1919. Hatton once again owned the building after it had been owned by several other owners and operators.

When it burned, it was the Palace Roller Skating Rink, a low green building with a tar roof that ended up "charred black and entirely destroyed."[10] The building was valued at $7,000, versus the $60,000 value of the Haden Opera House when it burned in 1901.

Even before it became a roller rink, the Airdome, like most theaters at that time, was used for much more than just movies. It was also a venue for events such as political speeches, religious ceremonies and graduation

The Airdome, which operated from 1902 until it burned in 1919. *From* Columbia, the Coming City of Central Missouri, *1910.*

events as well as vaudeville and dramatic theater productions. Like all public places until the 1950s–60s, it was segregated—although for a short time one of its owners barred Black patrons.

## ON THE MOVE

Its move from Sixth and Seventh Streets on Broadway to Walnut brought the Airdome closer to the other movie theaters on North Ninth Street that were popping up in Columbia, something especially important given that most people were on foot.

In March 1909, Hatton updated the Airdome with a steel skeleton, a canvas roof and seats instead of benches.[11] The ads touted its two thousand seats. In May 1909, the Airdome ran ads for a grand reopening, calling it "A Show With Some Class. The Tolson Stock Co. Bessie Burnell's Ladies Orchestra." Tickets cost twenty, thirty or forty cents and were free for ladies on Monday nights.

The free ladies' nights reflected movie theater owners' efforts to improve the image of movie houses with the public. People were worried about men and women spending time together in the dark during movies, and theaters were seen as places frequented by petty criminals.

## FOOTBALL COMES TO THE SCREEN

In 1913, the building gained a new name and a new game. Now named the Hippodrome, it began showing films of the Missouri-Kansas football game. An ad proclaimed, "The Kick that Beat Kansas," and noted patrons could hear the University Glee Club sing. The Hippodrome had new prices and a new slogan. Tickets were five cents, and the ad encouraged patrons to "Get the Hipp Habit."

In 1915, the former Airdome got an upgrade and, unfortunately, an uptick in racism. An October 14, 1915 newspaper ad announced the new management of J. Willard Ridings and O.S. Fuqua with promises of a thorough cleaning of the building, improved ventilation and "heat...so it will be comfortable on the coldest day this winter." The notice also said, "Negros not admitted." Prices were now ten cents for the entire first floor and five cents for the balcony.[12]

## W.B. GAGE TAKES OVER

Less than a month later, W.B. Gage took over the Hippodrome and renamed it the Walnut Street Theatre. He was also in charge of the Nickelodeon and the former "M" Theatre, but he wasn't really cut out for the challenges of the business.

Gage came to Columbia as a telegraph operator and a former railroad station agent. He was more of a family man than a movie theater mogul—a newspaper profile reported that he invented the lazy Susan, a patented ball-bearing and revolving table, to save his wife from having to serve him dinner.[13]

He set the prices at ten cents and advertised "Good Clean Vaudeville and Select Picture Programs." Gage did his best to keep his promise, including in February 1916 when he threatened to shut down the theater after chorus girls left the stage and rushed the audience to kiss some patrons. Gage blustered in a newspaper article, "No crowd of chorus girls can walk down the aisles of this theater as long as I am proprietor and insult my patrons by kissing them. I have lived in Columbia for five years now and have always tried to be a respectable citizen."[14]

Yet Gage seemed to struggle with staying on the high ground. By April 1916, he was showing what were called "hygiene" movies at the Walnut Street Theatre. Such movies involved sexually oriented themes or images under the pretext of a morality message or a public health concern. For example, the movie *Damaged Goods* depicts the results of a sexually transmitted disease, and an ad for it described it as "a stirring plea for pure life before marriage, in order to make impossible the transmission of hereditary taints to future generations."

But such movies drew crowds, and Gage said he was forced to show them. But he added he would only show one more and planned to close the theater.[15]

## TROUBLES AHEAD

B.E. Hatton, the owner of the Airdome. From the book *Columbia Missouri Herald 25th Anniversary, 1870–1895.* Collections of the Boone County Historical Society.

On August 16, 1916, the new Hall Theatre opened with 1,287 seats, modern ventilation and plush seats, giving the former Airdome stiff competition. Then in 1917, the United States entered World War I, and as college students joined the military forces, movie theaters lost a significant part of their audience.

By January 1917, the Airdome had a new name, the Palace Roller Skating Rink. Skating spots were gaining popularity, inspired by the 1916 Charlie Chaplin silent movie *The Rink.*

Its life as a movie theater was over, and soon its life as an entertainment venue ended as well.

In October 1918, the influenza pandemic hit Boone County, which led to closures of entertainment halls. The virus claimed the lives of 147 people in Boone County before the outbreak was considered over in February 1919. Hatton, who had retained the ownership of the building, lost his only son, Edward Bernard Hatton, to the pandemic in October 1918.

When the fire hit on February 18, 1919, there was little of a theater left, and the Airdome—along with its other names, the Hippodrome, Walnut Street Theatre and the Palace Roller Skating Rink—faded into history.

As for Hatton, who always claimed he started Columbia's first movie venue, he kept working, as he always had, in the paint and wallpaper business until his death at eighty-five in 1948.

# 4

# NICKELODEON, 1904–1921

## FROM HAT STORE TO MOVIE THEATER

Columbia's third venue for movies, the Nickelodeon, opened around 1904 in a building that was the post office in 1895 and then became a hat shop before transitioning into a movie theater.[16]

It closed as the Broadway Odeon in 1921, and along the way, the 1010 East Broadway movie house was called the Nickel, the Broadway Nickel, the Odeon and the Odeon Theatre. These names stem from the words *odeon*, which refers to a building used for entertainment, and *nickel*, which reflects the cost of a movie ticket at the time.

Rex P. Barrett and his father bought the movie house in 1921, renamed it the Cozy and gave it a complete makeover. The Cozy is covered in a later chapter from its opening to its closure in 1926, when Barrett sold it to Tom C. Hall, the owner of Hall Theatre, who closed it in 1927. After being used for retail, in 1935, the same building once again became a movie theater, the Uptown, which is also covered in its own chapter. Today, the building houses Slackers, a retail shop that sells movies on DVD or Blu-ray as well as music, video games and comics. A portion of the building has been used as a restaurant as well as an art shop over the years.

### WOMEN'S HISTORY HERE

As an early movie theater, the Nickelodeon made history as the first and one of only two movie theaters in Columbia to be owned by a woman. Originally owned and operated by Mrs. Joseph (Della) Craigo in 1904, at that time, like other early movie venues, the Nickelodeon had benches instead of seats.

The Nickelodeon's other claim to fame is its label as "Columbia's first permanent structure designed exclusively for motion pictures," versus the Haden Opera House or the Airdome.[17] Recall the Haden had been a dramatic theater and the Airdome an open-air vaudeville venue. The Nickelodeon was also always Columbia's smallest movie theater, even after its 1935 expansion from 250 seats to 703 seats.

By 1908, O.B. Wilson and I.A. Victor were in charge of the Broadway Odeon. The two men would eventually own or operate both the "M" Theatre and the Star Theatre, and both left the movie theater business after just a few years.

## COLOR AT THE MOVIES

In 1908, the movie house, renamed the Nickel, showed Columbia's first color motion picture. It was a short film, and each frame was literally "colored by European artists." The showing commanded the premium price of ten cents, twice the usual cost of a nickel.[18]

By this time, movies had moved beyond brief clips of a kiss or a train stop, but feature-length movies were a long way off.

Yet movies remained novel enough that an October 8, 1908 newspaper article explained to readers what a moving picture show entailed: "The average performance is thirty minutes. Seeing a moving picture show affords one much the same sensation as seeing—or hearing—the play of a football or baseball game shouted through a megaphone or watching a mimic yacht race." One movie "showed babies in a nursery, being fed and bathed," and theater drew many regular "first-nighter" students, who went to the movies "every time the program is changed, which was three times a week."[19]

But what movies lacked in storytelling, they made up for it with several accompanying vaudeville acts that might include dancers, singers, acrobats, magic shows or even lectures by local or visiting celebrities.

In 1909, the reasonable fear of fires led to many movie theaters updating their buildings to make them more fireproof. At the now named Broadway Odeon, this meant making the "machine booth," or the projector room, fireproof. At the time, all movie film was flammable; safety film wouldn't appear until the 1950s. Other fireproofing at the Odeon included adding two more exits, exit signs and a separate circuit to light the exit signs.[20]

Finally, the Broadway Odeon banned Black patrons from admittance. As noted, theaters were segregated until the 1950s–60s, and the Broadway Odeon lacked a balcony to accommodate segregated seating.

## NEWSREELS ARRIVE, MUSICIANS GO

In 1911, the Broadway Odeon was the first Columbia theater to show newsreels, and the theater announced it would show "a weekly review of the world's events by the Pathe film company."[21] At the same time, movie theaters were phasing out orchestras and replacing them with one or two musicians to play the piano and the drum. The smaller number of musicians could keep an eye on the movie and quickly change tempo and tone to follow the action, something an orchestra couldn't do, and it saved movie theater owners money.

As movies' popularity skyrocketed, theater owners cashed in.

A 1911 newspaper article declared, "Outside the banks there is probably no business house in town that handles as much cash as the leading moving picture [theater]," adding, "About 3,500 men, women and children attend the average daily performances of the moving picture shows in Columbia."[22] This estimated attendance was recorded at a time when Columbia's population was 9,662.

People may have flocked to the movies, but apparently, they also complained about the quality of the vaudeville that accompanied them. Victor and Wilson replied to such complaints in a February 25, 1912 ad:

> *Much that theatre managers and booking agencies do toward the uplifting of vaudeville is practically unknown to the public—little are their efforts appreciated.... An audience usually blames the manager for a lower class show when if they stopped to think it would occur to them that a theatre could not make money if displeasing shows were continually billed.... We are in the business to make money. How can we accomplish it unless we please?* Think this over.[23]

Shortly after this, Victor sold his movie theater investments and moved to Bexar, Texas. By 1920, he was selling insurance in that state, and he remained in that business and location until his 1946 death.

Wilson was then in charge, and he, like Victor, would soon leave the movie theater business, but not before he built the Hall Theatre in 1916 for Hall, his longtime friend and business associate. The two of them had been in business together in Centralia since 1892. In 1908, Wilson got his start in the movie business with Hall's half brother Homer Gray Woods. While Hall and Woods would remain in the movie business their whole lives, Wilson left it behind after 1916 to become vice president of Central Bank in Columbia.

In 1915, Wilson sold the Broadway Odeon to Gage, who then also owned the former Airdome and the former "M" Theatre. The next year, Gage faced tough competition with the opening of the massive Hall Theatre. He responded by renaming the Nickelodeon the Odeon, installing "roomy chairs" to replace the benches and closing the "M" Theatre on Ninth Street, so he could concentrate on the Odeon.[24]

Gage also showed hygiene movies at the Odeon, just as he did at the former Airdome, and faced the same complaints—and continued to scold the public via newspaper ads. But Gage didn't keep the Odeon long. First, movie theaters were hit in 1918 by war efforts to save fuel that led to closing theaters, saloons, pool halls and dance halls two extra days a week and after 10:00 p.m. The order eased a week later to closing the theater only one extra day a week.[25]

Next, as noted, movie theaters were closed periodically as part of the city's efforts to limit the spread of the 1918 flu pandemic. That fall, Gage joined the war effort and used his telegraph background to teach a signal corps class at the university. In the spring of 1919, Gage sold his interest in the Broadway Odeon and moved to Muskogee, Oklahoma, where he returned to working as a telegraph operator.

## BIRTH OF A NATION

In April 1919, two St. Louis men, J.D. Jameson and J.C. Ragland, bought the theater,[26] and in May they announced they would be showing the popular but now acknowledged racist movie *Birth of a Nation*.[27] This would be the second showing of the film—it first ran in 1916 in the Columbia Theatre, despite protests at that time from the Black community that the movie could lead to racial strife. (See the chapter on the Columbia Theatre for more information.)

Jameson's ownership and plan to show this money-making film marked the shift to movie theater owners who knew they had to market their theater and that meant showing controversial films. The days of just any flickering image drawing a crowd were over. The novelty had worn off.

Then in 1921, the Broadway Odeon was sold to Rex P. Barrett, who named it the Cozy and turned it into a marketing marvel.

# 5

# COLUMBIA THEATRE, 1907–1929

## DRAMATIC THEATER TO MOVIE HOUSE TO LAUNDRY

L ike the Haden Opera House, the Columbia Theatre began life as a dramatic theater, but by 1915 it had switched to mainly showing movies. A 1929 fire ended its life as a movie theater.

After that, the once grand three-story limestone building at 1101 East Broadway spent decades housing the Tiger Laundry until the 1950s, when there was talk of renovating the building and taking it back to its movie theater past, but nothing came of it. Today, the building, roughly across from the intersection of Hitt Street with Broadway, is missing its top two floors and houses lawyers' offices.

It opened on March 12, 1907, with a New York City play. It was built by J.W. Stone and W.W. Garth Jr., according to a July 31, 1951 article in the *Columbia Daily Tribune*.[28] Stone's only son, J. Dozier Stone, would go on to build the Missouri Theatre in 1928.

When the Columbia Theatre opened, coverage of the 1,047-seat theater described its exits as so "perfectly arranged that in case of accident it could be emptied in two minutes."[29]

In the end, that perfect arrangement didn't matter.

The March 3, 1929 fire that destroyed the theater started in the basement. A malfunctioning furnace was blamed, just as in the case of the Haden Opera House fire. The damage was estimated at $25,000, an amount worth $393,560 in 2021 dollars.[30] By then, it was owned by Hall, who also owned the Hall Theatre on South Ninth Street. At first, he said he'd rebuild and

The Columbia Theatre, 1907. The dramatic theater venue was partially destroyed by a fire in 1929. *Collections of the State Historical Society of Missouri.*

renovate it; then in April, he announced he'd be selling it for retail space. By this time, Hall owned the Hall and the Varsity, and at the end of May 1929, he would be part of the newly founded College Theatre Corp., which would run all three Ninth Street movie places, including the Hall, Varsity and the new Missouri Theatre.

## PLAYS TO MOVIES

For years, plays and concerts at the Columbia Theatre drew huge crowds, with special trains running from Centralia to Columbia to bring patrons to the performances. Newspaper notices assured theatergoers the trains would be delayed until after the play was over so they could get home.

But as the years went by, movies became more popular and the Columbia Theatre began to show photoplays more frequently. The reason behind the change was simple: money.

Plays cost more money to put on, and the expenses included scenery, costumes and wages for everyone from the performers to the theater crew. Also, each time a play was performed, the wages were incurred again, in contrast to movies, which could be shown repeatedly without any additional costs.

The price of theater tickets to plays was higher, with prices at the Columbia Theatre ranging from $0.50 to $1.50 for performances hailing from New York or Chicago. Ticket prices for locally produced plays and performances ranged from $0.10 to $0.75. In contrast, movie tickets ranged from $0.05 to $0.25.

To put ticket costs into perspective, in 1905, the average wage was $10.05 a week, according to U.S. Census data. That means a $1.50 ticket for a play equaled roughly one-tenth of the average weekly wage. In terms of buying power, that same price, $1.50, would be worth $41.17 in 2019, and the $0.05 movie ticket was worth $1.37 in 2019.

It wasn't just that films that made money. As noted, controversial films made even more money.

In September 1910, the Columbia Theatre scheduled a two-day run of the film of the July 4, 1910 boxing match during which Jack Johnson, the first Black heavyweight world champion, won against the white favorite, Jim Jeffries. The Columbia Theatre was the only venue in Columbia to show the match filmed in Reno, Nevada—and didn't show it until months after the event.

The delay in showing the film may have been to minimize the chance of violence. Immediately following the match, race riots broke out in twenty-five states and fifty cities, including St. Louis, Little Rock, New York, Pittsburgh, Philadelphia, New Orleans, Atlanta and Houston.

For the boxing match film, Columbia Theatre charged $0.25 a seat and offered two showings a day. That translates to an income of roughly $1,047 over two days if the house sold out, $28,185 in 2021 dollars. Also recall, if Black people wanted to see the boxing match or any film at all, they would have had to sit in the balcony due to segregation.

Given these facts, it's easy to see why Columbia Theatre phased out performances and announced on September 14, 1915, that the theater's fall season would begin with "moving pictures."

In May 1916, the Columbia Theatre decided to cash in with another controversial film with the city's first screening of *The Birth of a Nation*, originally released as *The Clansman*. Then and now, the movie is noted for its landmark techniques and quality —and as an effort to redefine the Civil War, reinforce racial stereotypes and herald the Ku Klux Klan as saviors of "the South from black rule."[31] It would be shown again later at the Broadway Odeon in 1919.

Columbia's Black community protested and presented a two-hundred-signature petition to Mayor J.M. Batterton asking him to halt its showing. Batterton responded by promising to look into it, and if the movie was as "the petition presents it to be," he would stop it from being shown. A newspaper article quoted "J.B. Coleman, a negro," as saying, "The picture encourages more violence, inflames hatred against the negro, and by doing so endangers his life and property."[32] In 1949, Coleman's son, Alvan B. Coleman, built Columbia's only Black-owned movie theater.

But the mayor didn't prevent the movie from being shown, and the Columbia Theatre showed it, charging $0.50 to $1.50 a ticket, an amount rivaling that of a dramatic play, and showed it for three days twice a day.

Despite the prevailing racism of the time, six months later, the Columbia Theatre hosted a performance of J.W. "Blind" Boone, an internationally known Black concert pianist and composer who lived in Columbia.

A few years later, like all of Columbia's movie theaters, the Columbia Theatre faced the problems of World War I, the flu pandemic that closed theaters and fuel shortages that closed all entertainment venues one day

At some point, the top two floors were removed, and today the Columbia Theatre is used as office space. *Courtesy of Deanna Dikeman, May 2021.*

a week and after 10:00 p.m., as noted earlier. But by then, the Columbia Theatre and the Hall Theatre were both owned by Hall, so the Columbia Theatre was kept open and the Hall on Ninth Street was closed instead.

Then, as noted, in 1929 fire struck and the Columbia Theatre's life as a movie theater came to an end. The stock market crash on October 29, 1929, heralded the Great Depression, and there wasn't any talk until the 1950s of reviving the theater, but that came to nothing.

At some point, the roof collapsed, and the building's top two floors were removed in a remodeling that left it a short, squat building. It is hard to envision it as a grand theater where dramatic plays and movies drew eager crowds—including a standing-room-only event in 1914 when activist Jane Addams spoke about the possibility of women voting.

# THE GEM, THE ELITE THEATER AND THE NEGRO NICKELODEON, 1908–1909

## THREE OPEN AND CLOSE

**B**y 1909, movie theaters had become a hot industry and five new movie theaters opened in Columbia: the Gem (which showed "Pictures That Talk and Sing"),[33] the Elite Theater, the Negro Nickelodeon—of all of which lasted about a year—and the "M" and the Star, both of which operated until 1916, when Hall opened the massive Hall Theatre with its up-to-date amenities.

The Gem brought an early form of "talkies" to Columbia, the Elite marked the city's last converted storefront operation and the Negro Nickelodeon was Columbia's only theater built, funded and planned by students—and the city's only theater for Black patrons only.

The 1909 movie theater boom stemmed from three factors: Movies made money, Columbia's population was skyrocketing and movies were a novelty. For example, the city's population grew 71 percent from 1900 to 1910 to 9,662 people. Movies were so new the newspaper published yet another article explaining in detail how they worked:

> *You drop into the darkened atmosphere of a movie picture show and you are likely to see a family quarrel one minute and a dog fight in Alaska the next. Small boys keep up a running stream of talk during the show. The other day one was describing a film called "The Greed of Gold," to a smaller youth. "See the villain? 'Cause he's got whiskers and a frown. He's goin' to do something mean. I don't know what. You wait and see if he don't. Here comes the pretty girl. The villain'll hide somewhere. There he goes behind the door."[34]*

The newspaper article outlined the costs and income as well, explaining studios distribute movies via exchanges that rent the movies to theaters for $15 to $150 a week and that a studio recalls movies after about six months.

Finally, the article explained "How Freak Pictures Are Made," describing how action films are made, film editing and other wonders we now barely notice:

> *To one who knows nothing of the practical side of filmmaking, the sudden change of a tramp into a fashionably dressed man is nothing short of miraculous. In fact, it is a very simple matter of stopping the camera while the tramp changes his clothes, dresses in his new costume and takes his place where he was when the camera stopped. The camera is started again and the miracle is done.*[35]

## NEGRO NICKELODEON: SEPARATE, NOT EQUAL

The Negro Nickelodeon, or "Negro Nickleodeon," as it was spelled in ads, opened in the spring of 1909 and closed nine months later. The movie house faced an alley that ran from Broadway between Seventh and Eighth Streets.

As noted, it might have seemed like a good investment, given the city's growth and the money-making potential of movie theaters, but Columbia's Black population growth was only 17 percent from 1900 to 1910, and its proportion of the city's population fell from 34 percent in 1900 to 23 percent in 1910.

The Negro Nickelodeon operated from spring to winter and then closed. It was managed by Woods, who had operated a movie theater in Centralia prior to moving to Columbia and went on to manage another theater opened in 1909, the 640-seat Star Theatre, owned by his half brother Hall.

Newspaper articles offered a series of reasons for the closure, including the supposition that Black people were not educated to appreciate "the flashing scenes, as thrown upon the screen. His vision powers, it is said, are not sufficiently acute." Yet, it offered a conflicting reason as well and stated theater managers had said Black people "do not like to be set apart from white folks."[36] Apparently, the writer was not aware that Black people had been watching movies in various churches since 1902, according to ads in a Black newspaper.[37]

The next spring, another newspaper article blamed the closing on "the pride of the negro [which] would not permit him to go up the alley to it," and then added, "They attend the shows at the opera house [the Columbia Theatre]. Whatever draws the largest crowd of white also draws the largest crowds of blacks."[38]

## THE GEM: EARLY TALKIES

Likely a storefront operation, the Gem operated for about six weeks from March to April in 1909. It was operated by "Dr. Rees and Casey, Proprietors," according to the ads, which also proclaimed it showed "Pictures That Talk and Sing."

Located at Ninth and Walnut according to ads, it showed movies using a Chronophone, a short-lived new technology. This 1901 French invention involved a two-step process. First, a performer was filmed lip-synching to a song played by a phonograph. Then a Gaumont Chronophone projector would link the projector electrically to a phonograph player. This synchronized the sound and the image. The Chronophone also magnified the sound to accommodate audiences of more than one thousand, although Columbia's Gem was likely a much smaller venue.

An ad in the March 29, 1909 *University Missourian* declared the Gem a success, and for six weeks it was. The Gem commanded a premium price, ten cents for adults, five cents for children, compared to the nickel charged by the Nickelodeons.

Until the talkies arrived in the late 1920s, movies added "sound" with an in-person announcer reading the titles, explanations or sometimes poetry between the scenes or with live music accompanying the film.

The downsides of live music included costs for the movie theater owners and matching the music to the scenes in the movie. The images and the emotion of a movie might change quickly from scene to scene, and an orchestra with lots of musicians wouldn't be able to change rhythm, tempo or tone fast enough to match the images on the screen.

As noted, some movie theaters switched to employing just one or two musicians who could change their music quickly enough to accompany the pace of the film, but then the challenge was how to supply all the sounds a movie might demand—from the drum of a stampede to the blast of a train coming down the track. Eventually, organs were employed to provide a fuller range of sounds.

The Gem may have closed due to the lack of available films, since in 1908, there still were only two studios producing the films, one in Paris and one in New York.

Or it might have succumbed to competition. At the time, Columbia was home to the Airdome, the "M" Theatre, the Nickelodeon on Broadway and Columbia Theatre; the Star was slated to open in November on Ninth Street.

The last mention of the Gem in the city's newspapers is an April 29, 1909 notice that the Gem's "moving picture machine" operator Fred Knoepfler was injured in a house fire at 615 South Fifth Street.[39]

With that, the Gem flickered out of history.

## THE ELITE: A TRANSFORMED SALOON

When the Elite Theater opened in 1908, any place could be converted into a movie theater. In this case, the Elite was in a former saloon, so little wonder its ads attempted to counter that unsavory image by proclaiming it catered to women and children.

The Elite at 13 North Ninth Street closed five or six months after its September 1908 opening when its manager S.G. Campbell opened the "M" Theatre at 8–10 North Ninth across the street. Campbell seemed to be as fleeting in the movie theater business as the Elite. After he announced he was building the "M," his name never appears again as a manager or owner of a movie theater.

The Elite advertised its opening with a few lines of text in the September 23, 1908 newspaper: "Visit the new Elite Theater. The best moving pictures in the city. We cater especially to ladies and children. Continuous performance. Admission 5 cents."[40]

Such ads declaring the quality of the movies and their suitability for ladies would continue for years.

The Elite was the city's second movie theater dedicated to movies, unlike other venues that offered plays, vaudeville and other entertainment.[41]

# THE "M" AND THE STAR THEATERS, 1909–1916

## BEYOND SALOONS AND TENTS

B y 1909, the movie theater industry had outgrown makeshift venues, and movie theater owners had caught on to two things beyond the fact that movies made money: safety and comfort mattered.

The "M" Theatre at 8–10 North Ninth Street opened in February 1909 above a warehouse. It had opera seats instead of benches and a fireproof booth for the projector. But don't go looking for this old movie theater. Its address is an alley behind the bank at Ninth and Broadway. The theater closed in 1915 under the name of the Annex after going through a revolving door of managers.

Yet this four-hundred-seat theater's claim to fame of a "fireproof" booth was important. Recall that at the time, the fear of fire was constant, with nearly daily reports in the Columbia newspapers of some kind of fire. After all, homes and businesses were heated with wood or coal stoves, making fire a constant threat

It offered vaudeville as well as movies, but the improved venue called for doubling the price to ten cents a person. By 1910, the "M" also touted its "new silver screen" and the length of the movie—three thousand feet of film.

## PLENTY OF VARIETY

Like most of the early theaters, the "M" featured moving pictures, vaudeville and live entertainment. Theaters were also used for everything from a Sunday

WAITING TO GET INTO A VAUDEVILLE THEATRE.

The four-hundred-seat "M" Theatre operated from 1909 to 1916. From the book *Columbia, the Coming City of Central Missouri*, 1910.

school lecture to fundraisers. For example, the December ad included the Buffalo Bill and Pawnee Bill's Wild West and Far East Shows along with vaudeville and a movie.

In 1913, the "M" hosted a "Tom Thumb" wedding, following a national craze of faux weddings of children put on as entertainment and a fundraiser. In October, the King's Daughters sponsored one featuring seventy-five children. "The affair is to be one of the society events of the season," an article proclaimed, and it named the luminary bride and groom as well as the other child attendants.[42] A later report stated it earned forty dollars for scholarships.

## GAGE TAKES OVER "M"

In March 1915, Gage took over the former "M," now called the Annex. Recall that he was also running the Broadway Odeon and the former Airdome, and in January 1916, he told the local paper running the former

"M" as well as the other theaters was too much for him. Gage said he would close the former "M" and remodel and improve the Broadway Odeon.[43] Four years later, in 1919, Gage sold all his movie theater holdings and, as mentioned, moved to Oklahoma—back to being a telegraph operator— never to return to the movie business.

With that, the four-hundred-seat Annex/"M" Theatre receded into history.

## THE STAR THEATRE: DRESS REHEARSAL FOR THE HALL

It's hard not to see the 1909 Star Theatre built by Hall as a trial balloon for the 1916 Hall Theatre he'd build in 1916 on South Ninth Street.

Opened on November 1, 1909, at 15–17 North Ninth Street, where The Blue Note is now, the 640-seat Star closed sometime after the Hall opened. And with that, Columbia's first movie theater built from the ground up as a movie theater flashed out of sight without a single photograph left to history.

A bit of that theater does still exist—a portion of a wall and the foundation were reused when Hall built the Varsity Theatre in 1927—which would later be transformed into The Blue Note.

When it first opened, the Star was leased to Wilson and Victor, who also ran the "M" Theatre across the street and the Broadway Odeon, and managed by Woods, who, as already mentioned, was Hall's half brother.

Victor, as mentioned, had managed the Nickelodeon, a converted store movie house, and now he bragged about Star's origin as a purpose-built movie theater. "I have been studying moving-picture shows all over the country this summer. The trouble with most picture shows is that they are placed in buildings which are not at all suited to the purpose....The public has come to demand that these buildings be better ventilated and be better provided with comfortable seats and exits."[44]

On opening night, the Star offered a cornucopia of entertainment, starting with the Star Orchestra, two "Staroscope Motion Pictures," the vaudeville act the Dale Sisters with "high-class singing and dancing skit" and an illustrated song by H.C. Cox finished off with a vocal solo by Mayme Reynolds.

While this might sound today more like a circus or a carnival than a night at the movies, in 1909 this was typical, and the movies and program changed frequently. An ad in the October 31, 1909 *University Missourian* stated the pictures would change triweekly and the vaudeville shows would change semiweekly. Tickets were ten cents for adults, double the usual price of a nickel, which had given early movie theaters their common name, nickelodeons.

## CROWDS COMMON

At the time, Columbia hummed with seven other movie theaters waiting to take the nickels and dimes of moviegoers, yet the Star didn't have any trouble filling its 640 seats.[45]

> *Led by the big, flashing electric star, you approach the theater and find nearly a hundred persons waiting for the first show to be finished. The crowd fills the lobby and overflows onto the sidewalk. On both sides of the street the curb is lined with automobiles. Along one wall of the lobby, under that glaring sign that announces "The Million Dollar Mystery," are a dozen baby carriages.*[46]

Moving pictures, the article continued, are the "most democratic amusement of today" and have "a strong appeal even in this academic community....There are nights when more people pay to see moving pictures than attend a Varsity baseball game on Rollins Field the afternoon of the same day."[47]

Sometime after the 1,291-seat Hall Theatre opened with its better facilities, the Star closed despite the usual promises that it would continue to operate. Then, like the Gem, the Elite, the Negro Nickelodeon and the "M," the Star blinked out of history except in the words of long-ago newspapers.

# PART III

# THEATERS BECOME DESTINATIONS

# 8

# THE HALL THEATRE, 1916–1971

## LET THE GOOD TIMES ROLL

The Hall Theatre at Cherry and Ninth was Columbia's first grand movie palace, a place where the theater itself was a destination.

Columbia's first movie palace opened only a year after the first such opulent movie theater had opened in the United States and four years before the 1920s, when the majority of movie palaces would be built. Eleven years later, Hall would open Columbia's second movie palace, the Varsity Theatre, which, as noted, is now known as The Blue Note. The Hall was in operation twelve years before J. Dozier Stone opened the grand Missouri Theatre in 1928.

Since 2013, when the restaurant Panera Bread moved out of the old Hall building, it has been sitting vacant, the grandeur of its two-story columns beckoning future redevelopment.

Now owned by Stan Kroenke's firm, TKG Hall Theatre, all that remains inside of the original décor are a few edges of the beautifully carved and colorfully painted stage of the now absent stage. The beautiful colored glass windows where a second balcony once existed are boarded over or are just dusty plain glass now.

The Hall stopped showing movies regularly in 1971, and before its career as a movie theater ended, it survived two world wars, the 1918 pandemic, the death of vaudeville and the birth of "talkies." The death of this movie theater can be blamed on drive-ins, multiplexes and the demand for convenient parking.

A 1967 image of the Hall Theatre, which opened in 1916 and stopped showing movies regularly in 1971. *Collections of the Boone County Historical Society.*

## OPENING NIGHT

The Hall opened on Monday, August 28, 1916, with a gala event that included speeches by local luminaries and showed, "two special photoplays and vaudeville." The Hall had taken nine months to build and cost $65,000 in 1916, about $1.5 million in 2021 dollars. The Hall employed eighteen men—yes, all men.[48]

Like all movie palaces, the Hall had a stage and all the necessities for putting on dramatic theater such as rigging, dressing rooms and an orchestra pit. The opening night publicity covered every detail and noted the quality of everything from the door locks to the orchestra pit lights. Even the lack of paint on the walls due to a wartime shortage was noted.

The orchestra pit was large enough for a twenty-piece orchestra and had a row of lights so each man had plenty of light. The lights, it continued, "are shaded with the latest orchestra rack shade." The opening featured a six-piece orchestra overseen by Professor Jack Whitney of the University of Missouri. The article coverage described the Hall's "music-cabinet…a modern installment" that put the entire musical library at the fingertips of the director. The orchestra pit was entered from the basement, where there were six dressing rooms "with running water and an abundance of lights in each one." There was also an outside entrance to the basement and a chute from Cherry Street to allow trunks to be brought into the dressing rooms directly.[49] This chute may be where the rumor started that there are tunnels under the Hall, but several sources familiar with the building from decades ago stated no such tunnels ever existed.

The Hall opened with $2,500 custom-painted scenery, which would be used for the vaudeville acts that would be part of the Hall entertainment until the 1930s. The movie screen, or "picture curtain," was selected personally by the manager, Woods. The projectors were "two new Simplex motion picture machines." Due to concerns about the danger of fire, special mention was made of the fireproof "cage" for the projector and the theater's twelve exits with doors equipped with "panic locks." In case of fire, these opened when pushed. [50]

The Hall also featured a state-of-the-art heating system and an early air conditioning system, which cost $6,500. Its cooling system forced air through "frosted pipes," where it was washed before it went into mushrooms placed under the seats. There were nine windows on the second floor that were designed to pull warm air out of the theater. The system was called the "most extensive and complete system ever invented." [51]

Like all movie palaces, the Hall had a balcony, and like movie theaters of that time, that's where Black people had to sit due to segregation laws. But at the Hall, Black patrons did not have to enter the theater via a side door or buy tickets at a separate ticket booth, as they would when the Missouri Theatre was built in 1928. Instead, at the Hall, Black moviegoers entered through the front of the building and bought tickets at a separate window in the theater's ticket booth.

Barbra Horrell, a Black woman who recalled those segregated times, said having to sit upstairs had its benefits. The theater's heating system with vents under each seat kept the balcony cozy.

## MAKING "TALKIE" HISTORY

The Hall Theatre was where the talkies debuted in Columbia on July 2, 1928, only a year after they had premiered in the United States. The Hall was the third theater in Missouri, after St. Louis and Kansas City, to show the movie *The Jazz Singer* with Al Jolson. In the movie, Jolson, wearing blackface, turns to the audience and says, "Wait a minute…you ain't heard nothin' yet." This was the first feature film with on-film dialogue. Within months, all movies featured on-film sound.

By September 11, 1928, the Hall had a "Sound Feature" policy, which meant it would show primarily movies with sound—and tickets would cost more. Tickets to *The Jazz Singer* cost thirty cents for the matinee and thirty to fifty cents for the evening showing. The new ticket costs were thirty-five cents for matinees and thirty-five to fifty cents for evening shows.

## HOT SPOT TO VACANT SPACE

The Hall Theatre, like all movie palaces, reflects a moment in history when stage productions and vaudeville coexisted with movies. Movie palaces with their thousands of seats are artifacts from a time when there were few other entertainment options and people rushed to the movies to see the latest movies and news.

As noted, in 1930, 65 percent of Americans went to the movies weekly. After television hit, by 1950, that number had plummeted to 35 percent. At the same time, people were buying homes in the suburbs rather than within walking distance of the downtown movie palaces.

From 1940 to 1950, Columbia's population grew 74 percent from 18,399 to 31,974, thanks in part to the returning servicemen and the 1944 GI benefits package for college expenses and home loans. Many of these families found housing in Columbia's suburbs, and that's where they wanted to go to the movies.

Soon Columbia would have three drive-in movies, opened in 1949, 1953 and 1965, an effort by movie theaters to make going to the movies more family—and wallet—friendly. But none of those drive-ins would be opened by Hall or the College Theatre Corporation, the 1929 chain of movie theaters created by Stone (the owner of the Missouri Theatre), Hall and Woods. For years, being a part of that chain had helped the big three theaters survive, but it never grew beyond the three downtown movie houses.

In contrast, the Commonwealth Theatres chain, which arrived in Columbia in 1935 when Rex P. Barrett opened the Uptown, kept growing. By 1953, it included the Uptown, the Boone Theatre and the Broadway Drive-In.

In 1953, Commonwealth leased the Missouri Theatre, and two years later, it leased the Hall and the Varsity. In 1955, Commonwealth encompassed all of Columbia's movie palaces and three other movie theaters, giving it control over six of Columbia's eight movie theaters. By 1966, Commonwealth had a suburban venue as well. Moviegoers wanted to go to the movies their way—where they lived, with more choices and easy parking. A single-screen behemoth downtown couldn't provide that then or now.

The era of movie palaces had passed away.

## A DREARY FATE

From 1955 until 1971, Commonwealth ran the Hall, but in May 1971, the company decided it couldn't justify the heating and cooling bills of a mammoth single-screen movie theater, even though it had been pared down to 725 seats during a 1960s renovation. The company pulled the plug so quickly it ran an advertisement on Sunday, May 23, 1971, for a film it would never show on Thursday according to Tom Mendenhall, who worked for Commonwealth at the time.

Ironically, the last regularly scheduled film shown at the Hall was *Zabriskie Point*, a movie portraying the unrest of the 1960s in America. After that, films were shown in the theater from time to time—like *Reefer Madness* in 1973—but it would never again have a regular schedule of movie showings.

## OPERA ANYONE?

From 1971 to 1978, the Hall harkened back to its roots of stage performances. It was used by the opera production class of the University of Missouri as a venue, producing and performing operas and plays ranging from *The Pirates of Penzance* to *The Crucible*.

A student at that time, Marty Loring, now a commercial trial lawyer, recalled the Hall's stunning acoustics. In a 2020 telephone interview, Loring said it was a fantastic place to perform.

"You could stand on the stage and you could whisper and someone in the back could hear you. We never had a microphone on stage," Loring said from his Kansas City, Missouri law office. "It wasn't run-down or dirty," he added, although the six dressing rooms under the stage no longer had the 1916-era upscale lights and running water featured in the opening night coverage.

"It was a fantastic place to perform, a big theater with tall ceilings," Loring said. "We were in heaven down there."

"It was an amazing seven years," noted Loring, who credited Professor Harry Morrison with his excellent training for some of his ease in his law practice. After all, he said, he never suffered stage fright in presenting an argument because he'd conquered that at the Hall Theatre.

## DREAMS OF A DINNER THEATER

From 1971 until 1987, various ideas about how to bring the Hall back were floated in the community. In 1974, Dennis Powell pulled a group together and thought perhaps funds for the country's bicentennial might be allocated to renovate the Hall. A May 1, 1974 newspaper article stated, "The building is sound and only in need of beautification and some remodeling on the inside."[52]

In the mid-1980s, a group of downtown boosters headed up by Ed Gaebler, director of the Downtown Business Association, thought they would be able to get a group of investors to bring the Hall back, envisioning a performing arts center. In a July 19, 1985 newspaper article, Gaebler said he had "several large theatrical booking agents" contact him.[53] But the effort faltered.

Then, in 1987, Garry Lewis, a lawyer and real estate developer who now splits his time between Columbia and Baton Rouge, bought the Hall and the Varsity. The Hall estate had offered them only as a package deal.

When Lewis bought the Hall, at first, he wasn't sure how it could be brought back to life, but he said in 2020 he'd hoped it would be put to use as a dinner theater and that's where he had put his energy. Lewis said he installed a fireplace in the former front foyer, leveled the flooring and made places for tables and chairs.

It was ready to go as a dinner theater when he sold it, he said.

A MU graduate, Lewis recalled the beauty of the Hall's art deco colors, the pinks and the golds, and was determined to bring it all back. Some things were still in the theater then, including the ornate woodwork and the chute for trunks to slide from the street to the dressing rooms.

## GEMS, SOUPS AND SANDWICHES

Lewis, describes himself as a developer, not a restaurant operator, so in 1988, when he had it ready to go, he put it on the market. He'd already leased out the other theater he'd bought, the Varsity, and Gary Grimes opened it as the Comic Book Club, a club venue for oldies music.

In 1990, Max Gilland bought the Hall, and he, too, believed it could be transformed into a restaurant. Or a mini mall. Or commercial space. From 1991 to 1993, Gilland floated various plans and said he hoped he could keep renovation costs to $250,000. At the time, the 1935 projector and the portrait of Hall, required by the deed to be kept in the building, still remained.[54] As of May 2021, research has not revealed the current location of the projector. The portrait of Hall turned up in May 2021 and is now in the collections of the Boone County History & Culture Center.

As Gilland searched for tenants, he continued renovating the interior. The sloping floor was removed, along with the seats, and photos at the time show steel beams being installed through the center of the stage opening, which would obscure the original vaulted ceiling. All remaining vestiges of the balcony were removed.[55]

In March 1993, Gilland moved his business, Bermuda Gold, into the north corner and basement while he kept casting about for possible tenants. Gilland's business involved making jewelry and selling gems locally and nationally.

In October, he leased out the main portion of the building to the St. Louis Bread Company, a bakery café.[56] Later, the sandwich shop changed the name to Panera, and it operated there until December 2013. By then, TKG Hall Theatre owned the building.

But no matter what Lewis, Gilland or TKG did, the Hall's role as a movie theater was over. Commonwealth sold the grand building with the stipulation first-run movies could never again be shown in the building.

## WHO WAS TOM C. HALL?

Hall made his mark on Columbia, building two of its three downtown movie palaces, but he wasn't a Columbia native, hailing instead from an Audrain County farm before he moved to Centralia as a boy. Nor did he ever live long-term in Columbia, only residing here off and on from 1892 to 1909. After 1910, he lived in or near Moberly until he moved to the Macon area before he died in 1947, only months shy of eighty-two.

On his death, his fortune was valued at what would be about $5 million in 2021 dollars and included the Hall and the Varsity theaters as well as all or part of four farms and ten buildings, including Booche's Pool Hall, the Huddle and the Model Restaurant.

His childhood was rough. The oldest of four children, he was close to his sister and his half brother, who was born after his mother remarried.

Hall was eight when his father was killed in a drunken fight.[57] A newspaper article said John Hall was killed "instantly by a pistol ball through the heart" and added both men fighting were "under the influence of whisky at the time."

Then a few years later, his mother remarried a man more than ten years younger than her, a union that didn't turn out well for Hall or, apparently, his mother.

After farming for a while, Hall's stepfather "Dory," or T. (Theodore) H. Woods, moved the family to Centralia, where Hall got his start in business in 1888 by going into the restaurant and bakery business with Wilson and his stepfather.

In 1892, Hall went into the saloon business with his stepfather and Wilson after building two buildings, one in Centralia and another in Columbia, with Wilson. In 1906, he bought another saloon, the Ringo Bar, in Mexico, Missouri. As noted, in 1921 he bought into the Columbia Theatre, and in 1926, he bought the Cozy, creating a three-movie-theater monopoly.[58]

In 1927, despite his promises to expand and improve the Cozy, he closed it that summer and razed the Star and hired the Boller Brothers, famed movie theater architects, to build on the Star's lot Columbia's second movie palace, the Varsity, now The Blue Note.

The decision for Hall to shift from buildings and saloons to movie theaters may have stemmed from money—or he might have been trying to escape the saloon business, an industry that had brought him and his family so much heartache.

After all, he'd lost his father in a drunken brawl and his bartender stepfather had no love for him. In 1926, when Hall's stepfather, by then a resident of Odessa, died, his obituary didn't mention Hall. Alcohol also led to the 1910 death of his older brother, who owned a saloon on Centralia's Allen Street at the time and died of alcohol poisoning after a week of drinking.

Or perhaps Hall sensed movie theaters would soon become even more lucrative than saloons. When he opened the Hall Theatre in 1916, the drumbeat was growing for Prohibition, which would run from January 1, 1920, to December 5, 1933. Outlawing the sale of alcoholic beverages would give movie attendance a boost and close down saloons, pool halls and other establishments.

Thomas C. Hall, the owner of the Hall Theatre, 1945. From the book *The Philosophy of Thomas C. Hall. Collections of the State Historical Society of Missouri.*

Hall's motives are unknown. His only published thoughts are in a slender book his sister, Maude Hall Jones, put together in 1945, just two years before his death, titled *The Philosophy of Thomas C. Hall.*[59]

A collection of short quotes, the comments seem to center on two topics: his high regard for hard work and his poor regard for marriage. The latter is unsurprising given what he'd seen of his mother's marriages. His mother's first marriage didn't end well, nor, it seems, did her second. Her 1909 obituary didn't mention her husband at the time, and they weren't residing together by then.

The book of Hall's quotations includes this reason for staying single: "Personally, I would rather be permanently seated on a hot griddle and fed hail stones from ice tongs than be compelled to spar for the last words. This is one reason why I have preferred a bachelor's happiness."

As for hard work, the book is filled with comments on its benefits, including this one that refers to his boyhood: "I want to say this, 'You can't get a dollar's worth of experience for ninety cents. The person who takes a shortcut to success generally has to back up and get on a regular route, as I did plowing corn, raising horses, etc."

The Hall Theatre is now owned by TKG Hall Theatre LLC. *Courtesy of Deanna Dikeman, May 2021.*

The results of that hard work remain in the form of the Hall Theatre on South Ninth and The Blue Note on North Ninth and the memory of Hall's role in Columbia's movie theater history from 1909 to 1947.

# THE COZY THEATRE, 1921–1926

## DAVID TAKES ON GOLIATH

I n 1921, Rex P. Barrett came to Columbia to attend the University of Missouri, and he had a plan: get a degree and use his family's business to support his college career and his growing family. His family business was movie theaters.

With the help of his father, Frank Barrett, Rex P. Barrett bought the Broadway Odeon at 1008 East Broadway in August 1921. He immediately renamed it the Cozy, and this time the name change would herald a new approach to bringing customers into the movie theaters—and later the first attempt in Columbia to show movies on Sunday.

For Rex P. Barrett, the movie business was all about promotion and marketing, explained his son S Barre Barrett. Even the new name of the movie theater was a nod to this approach. Rex P. Barrett faced the problem of luring people to Columbia's oldest movie theater, a tiny place with only 250 seats, versus the massive, upscale Hall Theatre, just a few blocks away. He was David facing Goliath.

Barrett's answer was marketing. The theater's initial ads capitalized on what could have been the theater's downside, its small size. The ads read: "Cozy Theatre—All the Name Implies."

He understood going to the movies was about more than seeing the flickering images. It was about how the movie theater itself made you feel, a lesson the movie palaces were driving home nightly.

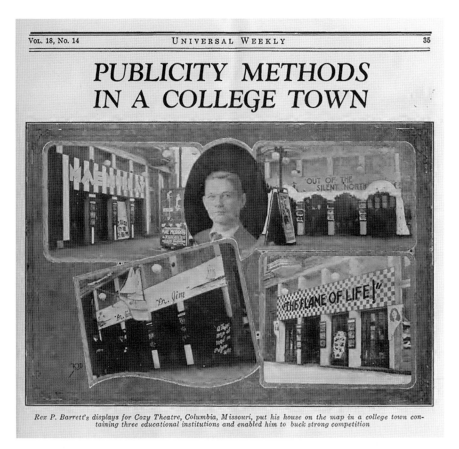

Rex P. Barrett's successful promotions at the Cozy Theatre were highlighted in the November 17, 1923 issue of the Universal Studios magazine *Universal Weekly*.

## EXPERIENCE AND MONEY

Like the other early movie theater movers and shakers, Rex P. Barrett wasn't from Columbia. But he grew up in the movie theater business. When he retired in 1961, an article about his retirement said, "When other kids in the area were playing marbles…Rex was running the gasoline engine that provided the electricity for his father's movie theater."[60]

That movie theater was in Granby, Missouri, and was named the Cozy, so the name of the Columbia theater may have been a nod to that theater. But whatever the origins of the name, the first thing Rex P. Barrett did was give the theater an update, redecorate and improve the ventilation.[61] Ads proclaimed that the Cozy featured a "Monsoon Cooling System."

Next, Rex P. Barrett updated the theater's "sound" system by installing a $10,000 pipe organ—an expenditure of $155,000 in 2020 dollars. The organ could provide all the music of a complete orchestra as well as an array of sounds, including sleigh bells, a tom-tom, a doorbell, a car horn or the ringing of a telephone.[62]

It also gained him front page coverage in at least two issues of the newspaper.

Rex P. Barrett knew he was competing with the impressive exterior of the Hall Theatre, so he put extraordinary effort into decorating the outside of the Cozy, which was an unusual practice at the time.

It worked, and his efforts and success were lauded in the trade publication of Universal Studios:

> *When* Out of the Silent North *was played, a white front was made of campo board covered with small bits of cotton and sprinkled with artificial snow. Results! Stood 'em up clear out on the sidewalk. For Mae Murray in* The Delicious Little Devil *a blazing red and white-striped front with bright blue lettering drew a full house. A front has to be different in order to attract attention in a college town, just as in any town. A prow of a ship looming out over the sidewalk was the solution for* Dr. Jim, *starring Frank Mayo. One of the surest methods of catching the eye is to display a large area of black and white checks. This was used successfully for Priscilla Dean's* Flame of Life.[63]

The piece said Rex P. Barrett showed trailers, also unusual then, and hired Wiley Paden, a University of Missouri student, to do the publicity and art.

On the downside, the theater remained an all-white venue, as it had no balcony, which is where Black patrons were traditionally seated during segregation.

## SUNDAY SHOWS FAIL

But one of Rex P. Barrett's promotional efforts flopped.

On July 11, 1925, Rex Barrett announced he would show movies on Sunday but said that "he had no desire to compete with the churches of the city," so his theater would only be open for the afternoon matinee and the 9:00 p.m. showing. The article noted, "There is no law in Missouri against the opening of theaters on Sunday, in fact, in the larger cities in the state the theater managers regard Sundays as one of their best days."[64]

Unfortunately, his timing was off. The Sunday he chose to start coincided with the city's Chautauqua, gatherings that had become multiday festivals, despite the events having begun as educational and spiritual events. Columbia's Chautauqua's program included six days of plays, lectures, music and vaudeville, including a "famous character impersonator," according to the ad in the July 25, 1925 *Columbia Daily Tribune*.

Barrett's plan may have hit the local Chautauqua organizers in their wallets. The July 25, 1925 ad said the local Chautauqua board had guaranteed the company putting it on an income of $1,500 and a quarter of the gate for any tickets purchased as well as half of any earnings above $1,600.

Ministers of the five major Protestant churches protested, saying they were against the "commercialization of the Sabbath."[65] No mention was made of the commercialization of the Chautauqua and the fact that it would be held Friday through Wednesday, July 24–29, 1925, including the Sabbath.

This church battle against Rex P. Barrett and his Sunday movies was one son S Barre Barrett said he would hear about many years later when the family recalled how when the minister at First Christian Church saw the Barrett family in church, his sermon topic turned to preaching against Sunday movies.

In August 1925, the churches adopted resolutions against Sunday movies, and Rex P. Barrett dropped the idea. Rex P. Barrett's failure may have been due to timing, or it could have been because his theater was the smallest in the city.

Note, the fight to show movies on Sunday succeeded in 1929, and by then, Rex P. Barrett was working for the College Theatre Corp., which as noted would include the Hall, the Varsity and the Missouri, representing a larger push for Sunday movies than the tiny Cozy's efforts.

## BARRETT MOVES ON, COZY CLOSES

In 1926, Rex P. Barrett graduated with his degree in business from the University of Missouri, and he sold the Cozy to Hall, who, as previously mentioned, then owned all of Columbia's movie theaters.[66]

On May 17, 1927, Hall closed the Cozy, and its last movie was Rudolph Valentino's last movie, *The Son of the Sheik*.[67] The newspaper noted this closing would end the building's career as a movie house—but it was wrong. It was just yet another retail break for the building that had begun as post office and a hat shop. In 1935, Rex Barrett bought and renovated the building and opened it as a bigger and better movie theater, the Uptown Theatre.

# THE VARSITY THEATRE, 1927–1972

## TODAY'S BLUE NOTE

Since March 1990, the Varsity Theatre has been known as The Blue Note, a live music venue that has brought nationally known musicians like the Red Hot Chili Peppers to its Ninth Street location.

This incarnation of the former movie palace by Richard King returned the 1927 building to its roots—music and entertainment.

When the Varsity opened on October 3, 1927, its first night featured vaudeville and an eight-piece orchestra made up of the "highest type of professional musicians...from all sections of the country."[68]

Oh, and it showed the movie *Camille* on opening night, too, but Woods, the Varsity's manager, was a former musician, and he would always focus on and retain a soft spot for music and vaudeville. As mentioned, Woods, the half brother of Hall, who built the Varsity, had been in the movie business since 1908. Before taking up the reins of the Varsity, he managed the Hall Theatre, Columbia's first movie palace. As previously mentioned, Hall's newest theater was built where the Star once stood, and the building includes a portion of a wall from that 1909 building.

In addition to being one of Columbia's two remaining theater gems, The Blue Note is where the Ragtag Film Society got its start in 1998, showing movies there before opening its first space on Tenth Street and years before it launched True/False Film Fest, an international documentary film event that brings thousands of people to Columbia each year.

The Blue Note is housed in the 1927 Varsity Theatre built by Thomas C. Hall. *Courtesy of Deanna Dikeman, May 2021.*

The building holds three distinctions. It is listed in the 2006 National Register of Historic Places North Ninth Street Historic District and the 2010 Columbia's Notable Properties list, and in 2017 it was named as one of the Cornerstones of Columbia by the city's Historic Preservation Commission.

## MORE THAN MOVIES

Mary Palmer's memories are different. They're not about the music or even the films at the old movie theater.

Palmer, eighty, laughs when she recalls going to the Varsity as a girl. Back then, during the mid-1950s, Palmer's last name was Bledsoe. When she was a young girl of fifteen or sixteen, she and her sister would go to the movies—but what was showing wasn't the most important thing to her.

"I went to the movies just to be going. To see my friends and talk," she said, adding with a laugh, "Today, I go to the movie to see the movie. I care what I see."

But back then, when she and her sister went to the movies, her father went to the pool hall next door. Then when he was ready to go home, he would come to collect his daughters. Palmer said they'd better be ready to go whether the movie was over or not. She said her father would come into the Varsity, stand at the back of the theater and wait for his daughters to join him for the drive home, no ifs, ands or buts.

But Palmer said she didn't care about the movie anyway.

"We had other reasons to go to the movies. I went to talk with my friends... and sometimes we did meet our boyfriends there," she said. One of them included Dale Palmer, a man she'd eventually date, marry and share forty-seven years with until his death in 2006.

But back then, a fifteen- or sixteen-year-old wasn't supposed to be dating and certainly wasn't supposed to be meeting a boy anywhere, and a movie theater was the perfect cover. Besides, the Varsity's upstairs lounge, an innovation when it opened, was the perfect place to talk—or meet a boyfriend.

Palmer's innocent gatherings took place during the mid-1950s, and by then the Varsity had started its long downward slide. The movies she watched—or didn't watch—would have been second run, and the tickets were cheaper there than at the Missouri, the Hall or the Uptown.

Later, its decline would include a stint as an antique shop, a cheese store and then a long vacancy, before King brought it back to life and made history there.

## 1927: BACK IN THE DAY

The year the Varsity opened, Columbia was bustling and jostling with businesses and movie theaters. It was two years before the Wall Street crash of October 29, 1929, and four years before Prohibition would be lifted, which meant people were frequenting movies more than taverns. The business buzz in Columbia included a groundbreaking for Columbia's third movie palace, the Missouri Theatre. It was a year before talkies premiered at the Hall Theatre.

Fancy. That's the only word for the Varsity Theatre when it opened.

Its decorations were Moorish and followed the latest designs in "motion-picture theaters, by emphasizing comfort and lavishments in decoration...."

The luxury of the theater makes itself noticeable the moment one puts foot in the heavily carpeted foyer."[69] The lobby was decorated in "blue and gold, from which any hint of garishness has been erased," with a mauve and blue ceiling with mulberry-colored columns supporting the balcony. The main auditorium was "tinted" a brown tone with warm-hued woodwork to avoid a monotony of browns.

The "lavishments" continued upstairs as well. The Varsity's second level featured a balcony, loges and a mezzanine lounge, which is probably where Palmer and her friends spent their time chatting in fifteen-year-old style. That lounge, the article states, was "something of an innovation in Columbia… and every fitting there including hangings, rugs and lighting fixtures is in harmony with the balanced decorative scheme."[70]

The Varsity was designed by the Boller Brothers of Kansas City, Missouri, a firm well known for its movie theater designs. The firm would go on to design at least one hundred movie theaters, roughly three dozen in Missouri, including the Missouri Theatre, and renovate several theaters, including the Hall Theatre.

The Varsity featured another innovation. It would show only movies on the first three nights of the week: Monday, Tuesday and Wednesday. The last three nights of the week, along with movies, it showed three acts of vaudeville on Thursday, Friday and Saturday. Sunday movies wouldn't come to Columbia until 1929.

The Varsity featured music, musicians and vaudeville long after its prime popularity, according to Harold Nichols, who recalled going to the Varsity in the early 1940s to see vaudeville and watch B movies.

While Woods focused on making sure the Varsity featured the best music and operating a good movie theater, the Varsity never shined as bright as the Star or its owner's namesake movie house, the Hall.

Yet the Varsity cost more to build than the Hall Theatre. It cost $125,000 to build the Varsity plus $10,000 for the lot, putting the price tag for the theater at $135,000.[71] In 2021 dollars, that would be roughly equal to $2.1 million, according to the Bureau of Labor Statistics CPI calculator. The price tag for the Hall was $65,000 in 1916, an amount equal $100,088 in 1927 dollars.

Yet the Varsity's façade is less impressive and smaller than the Hall's. When it opened, the Varsity featured 1,100 seats compared to the Hall's 1,291 seats, and its dressing rooms, orchestra pit and other amenities were far less posh. In short, it was a workingman's movie theater, a home for B movies—and music.

Even its opening fanfare was muted. While the rollout for the Hall consumed days of pre-opening publicity and articles in the local newspapers, the opening of the Varsity enjoyed a few front-page newspaper articles but nothing like the wall-to-wall coverage of the Hall. Unlike the Hall's opening, local luminaries were not on hand to give speeches, nor did the local business club hold a benefit there the first night. Perhaps movies and movie theaters had become part of Columbia's culture and were no longer the oddity they used to be.

Other explanations could be the fact that its 1927 opening was only a few years before the 1929 crash, and perhaps Hall, the owner of the Hall and the Varsity, was growing cautious and saw the economy as overheated. Or perhaps he didn't want the Varsity to outshine his namesake and legacy building, the Hall.

The Varsity offered several innovations, but it also included features traditional in Columbia: racism. An article outlining the opening night schedule stated the Varsity "will be for whites only," and in the future, a division might be made later for "colored and whites," according to management.[72]

Typically, such racism was understood and rarely made public in print. At the Hall, opening announcements noted that Black patrons would be seated in the balcony, just as in the Columbia Theatre. As noted, the Broadway Odeon had never allowed Black moviegoers, nor had the Star.

## WHAT HAPPENED TO THE VARSITY?

So how did the Varsity end up underused and periodically vacant from 1972 until 1990?

As noted, in 1948, television hit and hit movie theaters hard. The industry fought back with drive-ins, but that left the downtown theaters with too many seats and not enough moviegoers. Next, as previously noted, the downtown theaters were hit with a triple whammy: people moving to the suburbs, multiplexes and suburban shopping centers that drew people and downtown retail away from Columbia's center.

In addition to the economic and social changes, the Varsity faced two additional problems: competition from the dominant chain in Columbia—Commonwealth—and ownership issues.

Since 1929, the Varsity had been part of the three-movie palace chain: the College Theatre Corp., of the Hall, Varsity and Missouri owned by Hall, Stone and Woods.

Hall died in 1947, Stone in 1948, and this left Woods in charge—sort of. A codicil to Hall's will stipulated his two theaters must be kept operating as theaters for at least ten years following death. This meant Woods couldn't sell them off or even change what the buildings were used for. Recall when Hall died and made that stipulation, the first drive-in, the Broadway, hadn't opened yet. It would begin showing movies in 1949. Before he died, Hall had no way of knowing the downtown theaters would end up struggling to attract the crowds of people to the movie theaters that he'd grown used to seeing in his movie houses. From 1944 to 1950, the number of people who attended movies weekly dropped from 60 percent to 35 percent.

The Varsity was also facing competition from the Kansas City–based chain Commonwealth Theater Co. Operating like a cooperative with local owners, it ran the Uptown, the Boone Theatre and the Broadway Drive-In and leased the Missouri Theatre in 1953.

## 1955: DEATH IN THE VARSITY

In 1955, Woods, despite the codicil, decided to lease the Hall and the Varsity to Commonwealth. He signed the papers the last week of June, and a week later, on July 5, 1955, Woods took his own life—in the Varsity.

Reports said he went to work earlier than usual, put a Colt pistol to his chest and killed himself.[73] A nephew found him at about 9:00 a.m., and the sheriff said the death was certainly a suicide. Woods's death certificate states it clearly.

Reports of his death noted that Woods said he had been in ill health for some time and had announced plans to retire.[74]

Coverage of his death reads like a history of movie theaters.

Woods started a career in entertainment playing the trombone with the circus and later wrote songs and music. He also played the cornet, trombone

Homer Gray Woods shot himself in the Varsity Theatre in 1955, shortly after leasing it to Commonwealth Theaters. 1923 photograph from the *Collections of the Boone County Historical Society.*

and bass and was a band leader for seven years. But, the newspaper reported, once he saw tents filled with crowds watching "eye busters"—as early movies were called—he went into the movie business.[75]

The newspaper stated Woods was known to Columbians as "Mr. Showman."[76]

Woods's start in the movie industry began just after the turn of the century, and for a while he traveled with a kinetoscope showing a "one-reeler depicting a railroad engine roaring toward the camera."[77] As earlier noted, in 1908, he started the Electric Theater in Centralia with a partner and later came to Columbia to run the Negro Nickelodeon. He had been part owner in the "M" Theatre and managed the Star and the Hall before taking on the Varsity.

Yet Woods was a steady man, in contrast to his half brother Hall, who lived in various locations throughout his life. Once Woods settled in Columbia, he remained at the same address all his life.

But while Hall was a businessman who happened to own theaters—Hall never listed movie theaters as his occupation in U.S. Census records—Woods listed his occupation as movie theater manager starting in 1910. He basically spent his life as Hall's right-hand man.

When Hall died in 1947, he willed his property to Woods and Hall's baby sister Maude Hall Jones. But in 1954, Jones died, and Woods faced a changing movie theater industry. When he leased the Hall and the Varsity to Commonwealth, the newspaper noted the chain now owned six of Columbia's eight movie theaters.[78]

Movie theaters had reached a turning point.

## COMMONWEALTH TAKES OVER

Commonwealth operated the Varsity as an ordinary movie theater from 1955 to roughly 1963, when the chain closed it down, blaming falling admissions and the high cost of heating and cooling it.

In about 1967, Commonwealth reopened the Varsity as the Film Arts theater, a place for movies that audiences were beginning to demand, films that were grittier or showed a bit more skin than you could show at the drive-in. For example, the former Varsity showed *Blow Up*, a movie by Michelangelo Antonioni with a plot that includes random sexual encounters, a possible murder and no resolution.

But then in 1968, the Motion Picture Association of America changed its rating systems, creating the general audience, PG, PG-13, R and X or NC-17 system. This opened the door to the creation of movies with more skin, more violence and more exploration of adult themes. This meant

From 1967 to about 1972, the Varsity operated as the Film Arts Theatre, shown here in 1969. *Collections of the State Historical Society of Missouri.*

that all movie theaters, not just art house movie theaters, could get away with showing films with adult themes. This made a place like the Film Arts theater less necessary.

In May 1972, Commonwealth closed the Film Arts, and it stayed that way until a young hippie entrepreneur came along.

## A SECOND ACT: SECOND NATURE

The Varsity's closure and the effect of Columbia's first mall created opportunities for small entrepreneurs like Michael Cochran.

The Parkade Plaza opened in 1965, followed by the Biscayne Mall in 1972, and retail stores flocked to the new shopping centers, hitting Columbia's downtown hard. Cochran recalled the city was littered with vacant storefronts.

Cochran saw an opportunity. He had come to Columbia in 1962 to pursue a degree in English at the University of Missouri, and after a few twists and turns, including trips to Berkeley and San Francisco, he came back to Columbia in 1967 and founded the Sound Farm, a band with a Midwest following.

But Cochran realized he needed more income and found he could buy furniture in Missouri and sell it at a profit in California. But the drive got old, and he'd started collecting items going for pennies such as 1950s cocktail shakers and other unique collectibles. He needed a place to sell these things. The Varsity was vacant along with an office space next door. After meeting with the director of Columbia's Commonwealth theaters, he rented the tiny office space for fifty-five dollars a month and set up shop selling lamps, old fans and other collectibles.

He called his new venture Second Nature and immediately had a brisk business. As time went on, he decided to expand into selling and refinishing furniture. He negotiated for the use of the lobby for display and then the entire theater for storage and used the stage to work on the furniture. For $125 a month, he rented the entire theater and then subleased the tiny office to a jewelry maker.

"I made money," he said, even though he had to fire up the old boiler to heat the theater. "Gas [to heat the building] was by far my biggest expense," he said.

In 1975, Cochran decided to hit the road again after he and his wife parted ways. "I had a sale, sold out my furniture and packed up my smalls," said Cochran. In early 2021, at seventy-seven, he lives in Springfield and still plays music, occasionally returning to Columbia, where he still draws a crowd. And that English degree? "I have written four books published nationally," said Cochran in an email, "and I still have a book or two I hope to finish."

## CHEESE BOARD: BEYOND CHEDDAR

In 1976, the Varsity got another non-movie tenant—the Cheese Board, a cheese store that would become a tiny deli operated by Christine King, then known as Kris King, and Columbia native Mark Neenan.

The idea for a cheese store grew out of the 1974–75 European travels of King and Neenan, where they'd encountered an amazing variety of cheeses. In contrast, King said, in the Midwest cheeses seemed to range from cheddar to Velveeta and not much beyond that.

When the couple returned to Columbia for Neenan to attend graduate school at the University of Missouri, King decided to open a cheese shop. King, a 1974 Stephens College graduate, and Neenan had a friend in Jefferson City who was selling the equipment from his cheese shop, and King took out a loan from her parents. With another bargain rental rate for the Varsity, seventy-five dollars a month, the couple was in business.

The shop was in the lobby of the theater at 17 North Ninth, while a jewelry shop occupied the small space at 15 North Ninth Street, King recalled. They made the ticket booth into a display window and used a downstairs and an upstairs office as well.

King and Neenan's shop offered roughly fifty to one hundred types of cheese from Limburger to a Missouri-made smoked cheddar. Slowly, they added crackers, fresh juices and sausages, and soon they were catering and operating a little delicatessen with a fresh juice bar, along with selling wine to go with the cheeses they sold.

In 1979, Neenan graduated and King wanted to go to Geneva to study international relations, so the two sold the store and packed up their gear. King received a master's degree in Geneva and spent her career in education. When she retired in 2020, she had been teaching nonviolent communication and mindfulness classes at University of California–Santa Cruz. As for Neenan, he retired in 2009 from UC–Santa Cruz after working at the World Health Organization and Stanford University.

So, did running a cheese shop contribute to their careers? King said they learned a lot about dealing with people, adding, "We had a helluva good time. We made enough to survive and to get Mark through graduate school."

When they sold the business, the person who bought it moved the cheese store around the corner to an Eighth Street location.

## LEWIS SAVES THE VARSITY

For nearly a decade, the Varsity sat vacant, until June 1987, when Garry Lewis bought both the Hall and the Varsity from Hall's heir. A developer and an attorney, Lewis wasn't interested in running the Varsity itself but wanted to see it back in business, but what business he wasn't sure. His ideas for it ranged from a community theater to a meeting room for the community.

In July 1988, Lewis leased the former Varsity to Gary Grimes, who reopened it as a venue for his 1960s band, the Comic Book Society, and renamed the Varsity the Comic Book Club. Grimes had left Columbia to work in the gas and oil industry and with its collapse, had decided to return to Columbia and rekindle his love of music.[79]

Briefly, music reverberated through the former vaudeville theater, but by February 1989, the club was closed. Pro Music's owner Jim Widner said, "They still owe us some money on it [the club's sound system]."[80]

The Varsity was closed. Again.

## A BURGER LEADS TO A REBIRTH

One day, Richard King was getting a burger in Booches, a Ninth Street watering hole, and Cullen Cline, a local attorney, told King he needed to buy the Varsity. King laughed and wondered how that was going to happen since he didn't think he could afford it. At the time, Richard King was running The Blue Note at its Business Loop location, a place he described as a dive. But Cline reassured King, "I'm going to get you in there. I know the guy who owns it."

Cline introduced King to Lewis, and the two men hit it off. Soon they struck a deal, a lease with an option to buy in a year.

A few months later, March 1990, King opened The Blue Note at its new location—the opening show was Arlo Guthrie—and at first, he was preoccupied with settling in.

He knew the building was a find. After all, that building was made for putting on music and shows, said Deb Sheals, a historic preservation consultant who wrote the documentation that put the building on the National Register of Historic Places.

"He was smart and lucky," she said. And so was Columbia, said Sheals. "It's very hard to use a theater [building] for something else," she acknowledged, and the best way to preserve a building is to put it to work.

Without Richard King, the Varsity may have ended up like the Hall Theatre just a few blocks away, gutted for reuse.

Sheals also lauded Richard King's approach to preserving and using the building. "He's kept the best features and made them useful," said the veteran of thousands of historic projects.

That's exactly how Richard King sees his efforts.

"It's a beautiful building," he said, "and I'll never forget when we made the decision to bring it back to as close as possible to its original condition."

Since then, improvements have included replacing the windows with exact replicas of the originals, replacing the balcony that had been torn out and finding appropriate seats for the new balcony. Then there were the costly expenses no one sees but were significant, such as replacing the 1927 heating and air conditioning—or rather cooling system. The old system, King explained, consisted of vents from the street that ran under the floor into vents above and behind the stage with fans pulling the air out.

And all these renovations had to be done as The Blue Note's income allowed. But the new building didn't just cost money, it also provided opportunities, said King. For starters, it's bigger than the old location, which ranged around 400 to 500 seats. The former Varsity started out with seating for 1,100, but with room for a dance floor, the bar and other amenities. The Blue Note can accommodate 835 people.

But the new building is infinitely classier, something King said musicians notice. After The Blue Note moved to Ninth Street, it hosted stars like Johnny Cash, Willie Nelson and Ray LaMontagne, singers who had graduated to bigger venues than the former Blue Note location. King is certain Cash wouldn't have booked a stop in Columbia to play at the old location.

King also brought the building back to the roots of early movie theaters by opening its doors to other uses such as fundraising events for organizations as varied as the Central Missouri Humane Society and the Moog Center for Deaf Education. Recall that early movie theaters hosted everything from celebrity lectures to Sunday school sessions to Tom Thumb wedding fundraisers.

The new location, said King, gave him opportunities to give back to the community.

## 1998 RAGTAG FILM SOCIETY

One of those other ways of giving back came along in 1998, when Paul Sturtz and David Wilson came to King and asked to use The Blue Note to show some independent movies.

King said he'll never forget the two of them approaching him. "They had this idea," he said, and its independence and outside-the-box approach reminded him of when he and his business partner Phil Costello started the original Blue Note. "Someone opened the door for us," King said, and he said he gave them "some kind of crazy stupid low rent" to use the former Varsity.

As the saying goes, the rest is history.

As previously noted, the Ragtag Film Society evolved to finding its own building on Tenth before moving to Hitt Street, and in 2004 the society founded the True/False Film Fest, an annual several-day documentary event that draws crowds from around the world.

Unsurprisingly, The Blue Note was one of the original venues for the first True/False event. As King put it, "The building is the gift that kept on giving."

## TIME MARCHES ON

After decades of running The Blue Note, King decided to pass on the legacy to the next set of hands.

On November 3, 2014, Scott Leslie and Columbia native and MU grad Matt Gerding signed the papers to buy The Blue Note from King.

Until the 2020 pandemic, The Blue Note continued to offer live music and plenty of it—as well as comedy specials, charity events, rentals for weddings and other special events—and movies. The Blue Note, Gerding said during a February 2021 interview, shows roughly ten to twenty movies a year, events he called "brews and views." The shows are not first-run movies but instead cult or holiday movies such as *Elf* during the Christmas season or *The Rocky Horror Picture Show* or *The Big Lebowski*.

"[Movies] are not a core business," said Gerding, "but it's fun to play around with the space." The Blue Note offers a digital projector and a quality drop-down screen.

Finally, Gerding said, The Blue Note also plans to continue to be a part of the True/False Film Fest. "We love being a part of that."

While business was curtailed during the 2020 pandemic due to government-mandated closings and early closings, The Blue Note held smaller events at a 150-person capacity, versus its usual 835 cap.

Gerding hopes to have full houses again by the fall of 2021.

Before the pandemic, Gerding said they had even dabbled in vaudeville with acts such as fire breathers in a circus format. And while they've spent money on improvements, including $300,000 for new flooring, a new sound system and other improvements, don't expect any uncharacteristic changes.

In 1990, the Varsity became The Blue Note, a live music and event venue. *Chris Lotten Photography.*

"We have zero interest of ever changing the historic nature of The Blue Note," said Gerding. He and Leslie own the Madison, Wisconsin 1906 Majestic Theatre and have an appreciation for historic theaters.

"Live music can keep these theaters alive and functioning, and as long as we are in that building, we're going to keep doing live music."

# THE MISSOURI THEATRE

## BUILT IN 1928, SAVED IN 1987

B uilt in 1928 by businessman J. Dozier Stone, the Missouri Theatre was saved from certain destruction in 1987 by musician Hugo Vianello.

But Vianello—and the Missouri Symphony Society—did more than save Columbia's largest and most expensive movie palace. They returned it to the glory of its opening night on October 5, 1928, as "the finest in the central states."[81]

## A MUSICIAN WITH A MISSION

The road back for the Missouri Theatre started with one man's audacity and a $1,000 check. Today, after a $10 million renovation and years of financial struggles, this gem is owned by the University of Missouri, operated by the University's University Concert Series.

As such, it is the venue for performances ranging from ballet to opera to classical music to classic rock concerts. The University Concert Series books roughly 250 events a year in the building. It has been the site of weddings, speaker engagements, dinners and parties. It has also been the site for movies, including documentaries at the internationally famous True/False film fest that brings thousands of people to Columbia each year.

In 1987, when Vianello approached the manager of the Missouri Theatre, the building was endangered.

Missouri Theatre. *Courtesy of Deanna Dikeman, May 2021.*

The company leasing it, Commonwealth Theaters, had threatened to gut it in 1982 and turn it into a three-screen multiplex, following the trend of movie theaters at the time. Citizen protests beat back the threat, but the theater was by no means safe.

The Kansas City chain had been leasing the theater since 1953, but by the 1980s, movie theaters across the country were facing an economic crisis—too many movie theater seats and too few patrons.

Recall that in 1953, when Commonwealth took over the Missouri Theatre, roughly one-third of Americans went to the movies at least once a week, but after television hit, by 1966, movie attendance had fallen to only 10 percent of Americans going to the movies weekly—a number that hasn't changed significantly since then.

By 1987, moviegoers wanted more choices and easy parking. Commonwealth tried to balance the numbers out, closing the Hall, the Broadway Drive-In, the Sky-Hi Drive-In and the Uptown, and shifting to multiplexes by opening the Columbia Mall 4. But Commonwealth still had too many seats. The Missouri Theatre with its more than one thousand seats was on the chopping block.

## HUGO AND LUCY VIANELLO: AN UNSTOPPABLE TEAM

Lucy Vianello describes her husband, who died in 2018, as ambitious and persistent.

"If he got an idea, he wouldn't let go of it," she said in a February 18, 2021 interview. She also noted she acted as his alter ego, supporting his plans throughout their sixty-seven-year marriage.

Hugo Vianello began his career in the 1950s as a viola player, and his conducting career began in 1955 with the Oklahoma City Symphony. Throughout the decades, he held positions across the country.

He also received scores of accolades along the way, including the Missouri Arts Council Lifetime Achievement award in 2006. After his death, the city renamed the east–west alley south of the Missouri Theatre "Historic Vianello Way" in his honor—the same route Hugo Vianello walked for twenty-eight years as the conductor of the symphony.

These career changes and moves meant that in the first years of marriage, they moved numerous times, said daughter Lili Vianello. It also meant Lucy Vianello's career as an elementary school teacher fell by the wayside. Lili Vianello said her mother was the behind-the-scenes person who kept everything going. As her father was running out of the house, Lucy Vianello would be handing him everything he needed, added Lili.

This partnership was acknowledged by honors throughout the years that were given to Lucy and Hugo Vianello as a couple, including when Mayor Darwin Hindman proclaimed June 20, 1995, as Hugo and Lucy Vianello Day in honor of the couple saving the Missouri Theatre. In 2015, the city's Historic Preservation Commission named the couple as notable preservationists.

In 1968, Hugo Vianello arrived in Columbia as the director of orchestral activities for Stephens College and quickly came up with another new idea—the creation of the Missouri Symphony Society. In 1970, he and Lucy invited fourteen friends to their home, and that was the start of the Missouri Symphony Society. The goals of the society were simple: to improve the cultural music environment by offering professional performances and to encourage and educate young artists.

In 1987, the society added another goal: "The preservation and use of the Missouri Theatre as a performing arts center."[82]

For the first few years of the society, Lucy Vianello said, its "office" was the files shoved under their bed. Later, the society graduated to a cabinet at their home.

Hugo and Lucy Vianello.
*Courtesy of Lucy Vianello.*

By 1987, the society had grown, had its own office and was offering performances with professional musicians, but it still didn't have a dedicated home to rehearse and perform.

"We were going from place to place to find somewhere to perform," said Lucy Vianello. Lucy and Hugo Vianello were batting around ideas, and the possibility of leasing the Missouri Theatre came up. Since they knew David Jones, then the theater manager, Hugo decided to go see him. Once there, Lucy Vianello said, Jones asked Hugo, "Why don't you buy it?"

As it turned out, Commonwealth had just put the theater on the market the day before.

Hugo came home and told Lucy about the idea, and she wrote out the $1,000 check to hold the theater. Hugo took the idea to the symphony's board—which promptly approved it. The contract was inked on December 28, 1987, and for $370,000, the symphony was the owner of the Missouri Theatre, with help from a note signed by Klifton and Barbara Altis and a loan from the Missouri Department of Natural Resources.

That $370,000 was quite a bargain. When it was built in 1928, the Missouri cost $400,000 to build, an amount that would have been worth $2.7 million in 1987 dollars.

## A CLOUD OF DUST

Those first days of owning the building reflected none of the past or current glory of the theater.

"The place was a mess," said Lucy Vianello. All the things Commonwealth hadn't known what to do with over the years had been stuck behind the movie screen and curtain installed by Commonwealth and left there. Dusting and cleaning apparently hadn't been the company's strong suit either.

There were also holes in the walls Commonwealth put in for support beams for the movie screen, the roof leaked and the building needed a new heating and cooling system.

"When we took down that curtain, a cloud of dust went up," she said, making it look like a bomb had been set off. Symphony members went to work cleaning, painting and vacuuming, including each and every one of the more than one thousand seats. "We had lots of help and lots of good people," said Lucy Vianello.

Finally, in 1988 it was ready for its first concert, and one of its first performances featured the internationally renowned soprano opera singer Leontyne Price. Lucy recalled being there when Price was rehearsing and Price paused and said, "The acoustics here are wonderful."

Lucy said they all breathed a sigh of relief. Of course, she needn't have worried. The building was made for the sound of music.

## STEP BY STEP, DOLLAR BY DOLLAR

From 1988 until 2002, the symphony along with the Women's Symphony League, which was founded by Lucy Vianello and Jean Smith in 1971, worked and struggled to renovate and improve the building piecemeal.

Lili Vianello recalled the financial struggles the organizations saw during these times, too. When the Missouri Symphony Society first took it over and before it was ready to occupy, her father, Hugo, asked his daughter to visit the theater twice a day to check the water levels of the ancient boiler that heated the building. She'd enter the building, go through the lobby and auditorium, then down two floors into what felt like a dungeon and check the water levels and leave, turning lights on along her path and off when she left. But at the end of a month, her father got a bill for the electricity that twice-a-day check had incurred, and the amount shocked him. After that, he told Lili to use a flashlight to light her way from then on instead of turning on all those lights.

In 1995, the Missouri Symphony Society also faced the difficult issue of past racism and what to do during the renovations with the Locust Street entrance. From the theater's opening until the late 1950s, Black patrons were required to use this side entrance to access the one-third of the balcony set aside for them.

That entrance lacked the plush carpeting or even, some report, painted walls or sufficient lighting. A separate ticket booth was crammed under the stairwell, just inside the back doorway, and Black moviegoers had to climb up dark, cramped stairs to the balcony.

In 1995, the society asked whether this artifact should be renovated as part of the theater's history or boarded up. Beulah Ralph spoke up when the question was posed and said she recalled those days of segregation when she was a little girl and her grandfather carrying her up those steps. At the time, she said, it didn't bother her—until she realized what it meant. "You can't hide history," said Ralph in 1995, and added she was pleased the Missouri Theatre owners had gotten input on what to do from the Black community. The society contacted the African American Cultural Initiative and the Frederick Douglass Coalition for input, and both groups recommended restoring the door and staircase as historical items.[83]

Today, there is a large metal sign on the outside of the building that outlines this racist history: "Lest We Forget Never Again! Until the late 1950s, persons of color were not permitted to enter the Missouri Theatre by its front door. Entrance was only permitted through this back door and then only for seating in the balcony."

Years later, in 2007, the symphony launched a major restoration that ended up with a price tag far beyond what the organization had anticipated, said Lucy Vianello. The initial cost of the renovation was set at $5 million, but the renovations soared to $10–$11 million, according to various reports.

The work was extensive and even included re-creating parts of the theater such as decorative plaster pieces. The renovations included restoring the chandelier, adding new bathrooms, installing a new sound system and heating and cooling system and replacing drapes and theater seats. The banisters that had been covered over by Commonwealth during one of its renovations were uncovered and restored as necessary. In addition, the lobby was expanded and an elevator was installed.[84]

On May 21, 2008, the Missouri Theatre, then called the Missouri Theatre Center for the Arts, reopened with a black-tie gala featuring multi–Grammy winning singer Tony Bennett.

## TIME TO REFOCUS

The Missouri Symphony Society struggled to manage the theater and raise enough funds for its activities and to pay for the renovation and the salaries of everyone needed to keep it all running. Behind the scenes, financial trouble was brewing. From the fall of 2008 to the spring of 2009, a handful of firms start filing liens against the theater property, and the theater offered a settlement to the firms to settle the legal action.

Finally, the symphony decided running a theater was too much for it and shifted its focus back to its original mission: education and performances. In 2011, the symphony leased the building to the University of Missouri with the final sale completed in 2014.

While Lucy Vianello acknowledged she, Hugo and the Symphony Society had literally saved the Missouri Theatre from certain destruction, she said that wasn't the accomplishment they prized the most.

Instead, Lucy said she and Hugo believed their greatest achievement was having brought good music to Columbia, a legacy that has continued.

## BUSINESSMAN J. DOZIER STONE

J. Dozier Stone could have told the Missouri Symphony Society how quickly a theater can go from gala opening to economic problems and his experience dated back to 1908.

In 1907, his father, J.W. (Josiah Wilson) Stone, built the Columbia Theatre with business partner W.W. Garth Jr. As noted, this 1,047-seat, three-story stone dramatic theater still exists at 1101 East Broadway in a smaller version of itself after a 1929 fire.

But in 1908, problems cropped up over operations.

The business partners were soon locked in a legal battle that Garth claimed was about Stone wanting his son, J. Dozier, to manage the theater. J.W. Stone denied the allegation, and the two men couldn't come to an agreement. Finally, the theater ended up for sale at the courthouse steps.[85]

The elder Stone bought the Columbia Theatre for $20,500 in 1908, an amount that would equal roughly $547,200 in 2021 dollars, according to the U.S. Bureau of Labor Statistics calculator.

The elder Stone was likely a determined man, and his background would have given him a backbone of steel. He'd been a riverboat captain on the Missouri River before moving to Columbia and during the Civil War served with the Union forces.

His son, J. Dozier Stone, was a late arrival to his family, and his father likely doted on him. When Dozier was born, J.W. Stone was forty-one and Dozier's arrival came twenty-two years after his marriage to Elvira H. Dozier and twenty-one years after the birth of their daughter, Mary Ann. Before building the Columbia Theatre, J.W. Stone served in Columbia as sheriff and county clerk.

After buying the Columbia Theatre from his former partner, Stone installed his son-in-law, R.H. Hall, as the manager. And it's likely he did, indeed, plan on getting his son involved in the management of the theater, a position J. Dozier Stone would take in 1919, a few years after his father's death. By the time the elder Stone died at eighty years old in 1915, the theater was showing movies rather than offering dramatic plays or opera.

This is a 1930 view of the Missouri Theatre, which was built in 1928 on Ninth and Locust Streets. *Collections of the Boone County Historical Society.*

Perhaps when the younger Stone decided to build the Missouri Theatre, he wanted to make sure he didn't end up buying it back on the courthouse steps as his father had.

To build the Missouri Theatre, in 1927 Stone formed the Missouri Building Company with himself as president. The other officers were H.H. Banks, vice president and treasurer, and Fred B. Beaven as secretary.[86]

Unlike Hall, who was a farmer turned capitalist, Stone had been involved in real estate and insurance since he began his career. At first, he managed the real estate his father had accumulated, but he also had dabbled in other businesses as well. Like Hall, he'd accumulated some wealth. In 1919, he owned one of the few automobiles in Columbia, although he seemed to be a bit shaky as a driver. Stone was involved in two auto accidents, one in 1915 and the other in 1919, both within blocks of the 1004 Conley home that he'd once shared with his parents.

And for a long time, it had looked like he might be a lifelong bachelor like Hall, until 1927, when Stone married at forty-seven years old. His son was born in 1928.

But no matter how much wealth Stone managed to accumulate, the days of one man taking on a project of this caliber were waning. The movie theater industry was growing up, and the days of converted saloons or dramatic theaters were fading.

The Missouri was one of Columbia's most expensive construction projects until that time and one of the most expensive movie theaters built until then. Only the Tiger Hotel, also built by a company, not one person, topped the $400,000 cost of the Missouri Theatre. The Tiger Hotel, a nine-story building, carried an estimated cost of $500,000 and also opened in 1928.

The 1928 cost to build the Missouri would be equal $6.1 million in 2021 dollars, according to the U.S. Bureau of Labor Statistics CPI calculator. As noted, in 1987, the Missouri Symphony Society bought the Missouri at a bargain price, $370,000, or roughly $838,695 in 2021 dollars.

The Missouri Theatre wasn't just Columbia's most expensive theater, it was the city's largest, with 1,600 seats. Of the two theaters built by Hall, the Hall (1916) had 1,291 seats and had cost $65,000. The Varsity was built the year before the Missouri, with roughly 1,100 seats, and had cost $100,000 to build.

## PLANS REDRAWN

Stone also faced yet another snafu even before the Missouri Theatre broke ground.

He had planned to build a theater with a six-story hotel above it, but when plans for the Tiger Hotel came out, that building was going to include a theater. Both companies decided to change their plans, and the Tiger Hotel omitted the theater while the Missouri Theatre skipped building a hotel. Stone, however, built the Missouri with a foundation sufficient to support the hotel he hoped to build later.

These projects show Columbia was caught up in the trends of the Roaring Twenties with big plans and big developments. Columbia was also growing by leaps and bounds.

From 1920 to 1930, the city's population grew 44 percent, to 14,967. Even after the stock market crash in 1929, the city grew 23 percent from 1930 to 1940 and skyrocketed up 74 percent from 1940 to 1950 to 31,974 people.

Prohibition also was still in effect, so in 1928, it looked like movie theaters would remain the city's main form of entertainment.

Big construction projects were so lauded during this time, no one decried the demolition of a historic home when the Missouri Theatre was built, though it did earn some press coverage. The house that was demolished had been occupied by G.D. Foote, one of the builders of Academic Hall, which burned in 1892. When the Missouri Theatre was going to be built, that house was owned by Robert L. Todd, first cousin of Mary Todd Lincoln. Todd was also one of the two men who comprised the first graduating class of the University of Missouri.

## WHAT DOES $400,000 BUY?

When the Missouri Theatre opened on October 5, 1928, it was so grand that apparently the *Columbia Missourian* reporter previewing it ran out of words to describe it. "The beauty of the house beggar's description and can be best told by seeing it," read an October 4, 1928 article. Fortunately, before he ran out of words, he called it "one of the most beautiful and best equipped theaters in the state…and…the last word in theatrical architecture."[87]

The Missouri Theatre was designed by the Boller Brothers, a Kansas City firm, which designed hundreds of other movie theaters in the Midwest. The theater boasted Louis the XIV and XV style in both color and design, according to the coverage. Other documents state its design was inspired by the Paris Opera House of Garnier—and the theater even has faux opera boxes to secure the impression that it is indeed an opera house. Two of the boxes disguise the alcove for the massive organ. At the time of its opening, the main colors of the interior were gold and maroon, newspaper reports stated. The woodwork was French gray with gold highlights. C. Bonfig Decorating of St. Louis was in charge of the interior décor.

"Indirect lighting is used through artglass centerpieces and a large dome, 28 feet in diameter. The main chandelier, hanging from the center of the dome, is composed of 300 lamps and has an estimated value of $2,000," the *Columbia Missourian* continued. Laced through the description of the interior were concerns of fire, warranted given how common fire was at the time and how flammable film was then. As noted, safety film wouldn't come into use until the 1950s. The reporting noted the building was fireproof and had thirteen exits. "The projection room itself is enclosed in a 2-inch solid wall and equipped with automatic steel shutters entirely closing the room in case of fire," the *Missourian* noted, adding that the stage had an asbestos curtain and large fire doors behind the stage. The theater's projection room had three projectors and provisions for both forms of showing movies with sound, Moviefone and Vitaphone, but "neither would be installed at present."[88]

The orchestra pit was forty feet long and eight feet wide, while the stage itself was thirty feet deep and thirty-six feet wide. Beside the stage were six dressing rooms six feet by ten feet, each with its own lavatory and toilet.[89]

The carpet was custom loomed for the building and included a special design with the seal of the State of Missouri.

## BETTING ON AN ORGAN

Stone had gambled on silent movies continuing and installed a $25,000 Robert Morton pipe organ, an investment that would be worth $378,000 in 2021 dollars.

Why Stone failed to install projectors for talkies is unknown. Recall that the talkies had hit Columbia on July 2, 1928, three full months before the Missouri opened, and by September 11, 1928, the Hall Theatre was showing talkies almost exclusively—and charging an extra nickel.

Perhaps Stone thought the beauty of the Missouri would command the same prices as the Hall but without the added expense of a projector for the talkies, because opening-night tickets were priced the same as the Hall's thirty-five-cent tickets for talkies for seating in the main auditorium and twenty-five cents for the balcony and matinees.

The press was smitten with the organ, and the instrument was used for the vaudeville acts that would continue to be part of an evening's entertainment at the movies for another decade or so.

"Theater organ is 'Full Orchestra,'" an October 4, 1928 article declared. This organ wasn't what most people envision when they think of an organ, such as a church organ. Instead, this organ could replicate the entire breadth and width of an entire orchestra of musicians playing everything from the tiniest drum to the loudest brass horn and everything in between.

*Seven hundred copper wires, which if placed ended to end would more than reach around the world, pipes ranging in size from sixteen feet long and eighteen inches in diameter to half an inch in length and a quarter of an inch in diameter, as many electro-magnets as pipes, a five horsepower "blower," a swell shade and tremulo apparatus for each set of pipes, are just a few of the thousands of parts which make up the mighty Robert Morton organ that will be one of the features of every performance in the Missouri Theater.*

The organ had taken a factory representative five weeks to install, and it included 215 keys and about 100 stops and could create "practically any known combination of effects."[90]

This pricey and amazing organ was simply set aside when vaudeville and silent movies faded in the 1930s and 1940s. In 1975, a Commonwealth executive bought the organ for $700 and sold it later. The Missouri Symphony Society tried to buy the organ back, but its efforts failed. Then in 1995, an almost identical organ was donated to the Missouri by Glen and Julia Spelman of California and installed.[91]

As of 2021, the organ is fully functional, and its intricate workings fills one opera box on the side of the stage, ready to provide the Missouri Theatre with the sound of an entire orchestra.

## GRAND OPENING

Opening night drew two capacity houses as Columbians took the *Missourian*'s advice about seeing the Missouri Theatre for themselves. Filling the 1,600-seat theater twice would equal one-fifth of the city's roughly 15,000 population at the time.

The grand opening program headlined the movie *Steamboat Bill Jr.*, starring Buster Keaton. The Missouri's "Formal Opening" listed the movie first; then Jack Keith, master of ceremonies and his Missouri Stage Band; "Big Time Vaudeville Presentation"; Bob Crowley at the console of the mighty Morton; Latest News Reel; Cartoon Comedy; Comedy—"Hollywood or Bust"; and finally, Novelty—"Believe it or not." It's reputed the vaudeville acts included then little-known comedian Leslie Townes Hope, who would go on to become Bob Hope.

Comparing the opening bills of the Hall, Varsity and the Missouri, it appears vaudeville was fading in importance. The Missouri Theatre's grand opening's greatest fanfare highlighted the movie title, with the other attractions listed afterward. In 1916, the Hall's grand opening ads touted "Special Feature Photoplays and Vaudeville." In 1927, the Varsity opening ad highlighted its opening movie, and five days later, its ad boasted three big acts of vaudeville.

The opening night went off without a hitch, at least as far as the entertainment.

One more mistake showed up in the *Columbia Missourian* newspaper. On October 4, 1928, the *Columbia Missourian* published a picture of the Missouri

Theatre—as it had been planned to look, complete with the hotel above the storefronts.

Yet even pared back, the Missouri Theatre included more than a movie theater. The complex included space for eight stores, and by opening night, five were rented and two were occupied. The stores included the Missouri Drug Store, Knight & Quarles Men's Furnishings, the Missouri Barber Shop, the Marinello Beauty Parlor and Paul Parson's Studio, the article noted.

As of 2021, the storefronts were occupied by the Columbia Art League, which held its grand opening in 2008, and Yogoluv, a frozen yogurt bar that opened in 2009.

## REALITY HITS

By January 1929, movie theaters were facing the same troubles as the Commonwealth would in the 1970s and 1980s—too many seats and not enough patrons.

The Hall Theatre opened in 1916 with 1,291 seats; in 1927, the Varsity opened with roughly 1,000 seats; and the 1928 Missouri added 1,600 seats to the Ninth Street trilogy for a total of 3,891 seats in a town of about 15,000 people.

At first, Stone fought back by switching to talkies. A January 2, 1929 ad in the *Columbia Daily Tribune* announced, "The first half of the week we will present the latest Sound Pictures and 3 acts of the Best Vaudeville. The second half of the week we will offer the pick of Silent Pictures and 5 acts of vaudeville." By April, another ad announced the Missouri would be showing "All Talking All Singing All Playing Syncopation" movies.

On January 8, 1929, the *Kansas City Times* took note of Columbia's movie theaters' troubles: "Columbia's theater war has broken out again. While the rival operating companies continue to 'fight,' Columbia's student population and its townspeople are kept busy hurrying to one of the four shows now running to see pictures and vaudeville better than has ever been offered here before." Noting Hall as the Moberly millionaire who controlled the Varsity, Hall and Columbia theaters, the article referred to the Missouri Theatre as the new $500,000 amusement house managed by Stone, the "Columbia capitalist." The article concluded, "Those in the 'know' here say neither Stone nor Hall are making money. But Columbia theatergoers [*sic*] are profiting."[92]

## THE COLLEGE THEATRE CORPORATION

The fighting between Hall and Stone ended on May 30, 1929.

Stone, Hall and Woods created the College Theatre Corp. and agreed the three movie theaters would be managed as one. Again, the company featured Stone as president, but now Hall was vice president and Woods secretary-treasurer.

In October 1929, the group looked for another revenue stream: Sunday movies.

When Rex P. Barrett, the owner of the Cozy, decided to show movies on Sunday in 1925, he announced his intentions weeks earlier to appease church pastors, noting the movies would be shown in the afternoon and wouldn't interfere with church services. But as noted, his timing was off and his Sunday movies attempt coincided with a community festival.

This time, the push to show movies on Sunday was backed by the College Theatre Corp., which represented all of the city's movie theaters. Also, they didn't warn the pastors but instead simply ran an ad on Saturday stating the Missouri would be showing movies the next day.

On Monday, October 7, 1929, the *Columbia Daily Tribune*'s front page included this headline, "CHURCHES PROTEST SUNDAY THEATRES."[93]

But between 1925 and 1929, society had changed, and movies were an entrenched part of our lives. The 1925 attempt at Sunday movies had drawn only a few patrons, but in 1929, a crowd showed up for the Sunday movies. The legal landscape had changed since 1925 as well. The Missouri Supreme Court had recently ruled any ordinance that singled out movie theaters for Sunday closure was invalid.

When the Columbia City Council met to discuss crafting a law to keep movies closed, city officials worried any law deemed valid would mean closing all Sunday operations, from ice cream parlors to dog shows. In a short time, the issue died down, and some might say moviegoers won. Eventually, all movie theaters began to show movies on Sundays.

## COMMONWEALTH TAKES OVER

Stone died on May 1, 1948, at sixty-seven, and his wife took over as head of the Missouri Theatre Company. Hazel Mayes Stone died in 1954, but she had already leased the Missouri Theatre to Commonwealth.

The Missouri Theatre, 1978, was operated by the Commonwealth Theaters from 1955 to 1987. *Collections of the State Historical Society of Missouri.*

By then, the theater business was in trouble, hit by television, the move to suburbia and the demand for movie theaters there, not downtown.

Commonwealth had arrived in Columbia in 1935 when Barrett opened the Uptown. The chain had opened Columbia's first drive-in, the Broadway Drive-In Theatre, in 1949, but these outdoor theaters wouldn't last or bring back the crowds.

Commonwealth tried to keep its downtown theaters alive and gave the Missouri a major spruce up, installing an improved screen and speaker system and modernized it by moving the ticket booth and installing a large pink and gold plaster concession stand on the wall below the balcony. There are some indicators that this was the first time the Missouri Theatre had a concession stand inside the theater. Previously, patrons had to go to the drugstore on the corner for snacks.

In 1965, another renovation took place and concluded with a grand reopening. The program for that night, September 9, 1965, included organ music with George H. Willhoite at the Hammond, a civic citation by Columbia Chamber of Commerce president Eugene F. Ruether Jr., an introduction of the 1965 University of Missouri football team by head coach Dan Devine and the movie *Shenandoah* starring James Stewart. The gala

This 1965 Missouri Theatre concession stand was installed by Commonwealth, reputed to be the first concession stand in the theater. *Collection of Barre Barrett.*

The Missouri Theatre's renovated interior. *Courtesy of the Missouri Symphony.*

event included the appearance of the University of Missouri cheerleaders and Pom Pom Girls.

The program called the Missouri the "undisputed flagship of the Commonwealth Fleet of 108 movie theatres" of the chain's holding from Missouri to Wyoming. But the end of downtown movie theaters was already in sight. In the 1965 program, Commonwealth noted the Varsity was already dark.

No chain of theaters can hold back the hands of time.

By the time Hugo Vianello spoke to the Commonwealth manager about the Missouri Theatre, the Kansas City–based chain had closed the Hall, both of its drive-ins and the Uptown—and opened the Columbia Mall 4.

The era of movie palaces had passed away.

But a musician walked in.

# PART IV

# COMMONWEALTH COMES TO COLUMBIA

# 12

# THE UPTOWN, 1935–1986

## A NEW BUSINESS MODEL

In 1935, Rex P. Barrett, the same brash young man who owned the Cozy in 1921 and updated it to compete with the Hall Theatre, took over the same location again, and this time opened it as an all new theater called the Uptown, and brought a new business model to Columbia's movie theater industry.

The Uptown opened on May 18, 1935, as a member of the Commonwealth Amusement Company, a chain of seventeen theaters in three states.

This newly formed company operated like a cooperative, employing local men to own and manage the theaters, in this case, Rex P. Barrett. Before it was folded into United Artists Releasing in 1986, Commonwealth became the largest movie theater chain—with 431 screens in twelve states—and dominated Columbia's movie theater industry. By the time it closed its Columbia operations, Commonwealth operated the Uptown, Boone, Broadway Drive-In, the Sky-Hi, the Cinema, the Campus Twin, the Missouri, Hall, Varsity and Columbia Mall 4.

Commonwealth's entry into Columbia marked a turning point in the city's movie theater history.

From this point on, an independent or family-owned movie theater became a rarity in Columbia. Recall that Hall built the Hall and Varsity and J. Dozier Stone formed his own company to build the Missouri Theatre.

The Uptown Theatre opened in 1935 and closed in 1986. *Collection of S Barre Barrett.*

## WHY DID COMMONWEALTH MATTER?

Commonwealth provided the Uptown with the most important key to movie theater success: access to a reliable source of good movies.

S Barre Barrett explained that when Rex P. Barrett owned the Cozy, he had to go to Kansas City himself to negotiate for films, and even then, he might or might not get the film, because at that time distributors were not reliable.

With Commonwealth membership, Barrett received films from Columbia, RKO, Universal and others, said Jim Ewing, who worked in Columbia for Commonwealth theaters from 1947 to 1951. His competition, the College Theatre Corp. group, made up of the Missouri, Hall and Varsity theaters, showed MGM, Paramount and 20th Century Fox films.

In some cities, theaters had access to movies because they were owned or operated by the big Hollywood studios, like the Fox Theatre in St. Louis, but Columbia never had a studio theater.

## A NEW MAN

Rex P. Barrett returned to the site of the Cozy at 1006–8 East Broadway, but he wasn't the same man he'd been in 1921 when he opened that theater.

He had under his belt five years of experience of working for the three-theater group, the College Theatre Corp., in the Missouri Theatre and a freshly minted doctorate in business from the University of Missouri. His dissertation focused on the business of movie theaters.

Rex P. Barrett also had a burning desire to succeed. After he sold the Cozy to Hall, the owner of the Hall Theatre, Barrett moved to Alton, Illinois, and tried his hand at owning a movie theater there. No one in the family knows exactly what happened, but it didn't end well.

As noted, he also had that deep-rooted movie theater love from working in his father's movie house in Granby. But S Barre Barrett said his father's greatest assets were his personality and passion for promotion. "My father was a go-getter and a showman. He always had some kind of vision, and he was always thinking about new ways to get people in the seats," he said.

That meant, like with the Cozy, the first thing Rex P. Barrett did was renovate the space for the Uptown.

He excavated the floor, creating better visibility, and put in comfortable seating to keep up with the plush surroundings of Columbia's movie palaces. He also expanded it from 250 seats to 703. It still fell short of the more than

1,000 seats of all of the city's three downtown movie houses, but it was no longer a hole in the wall. The theater included a shallow orchestra pit in front of the screen, according to Ted Pettit, Rex Barrett's grandson.

Next, Rex P. Barrett gave the building a striking new look. He knew the outside mattered as much as the movies showing inside. The Uptown's exterior was a sharp contrast with Columbia's three other movie theaters. Instead of the stately looks of the Hall or the Missouri, the Uptown looked like it was going to take off into the next century. Beautiful yellow and green glittering panels rose above the marquee, making the ground floor look as if it rose above the street.

The movie theater occupied the first floor of the building, and the basement housed a lounge, restrooms, storage and office space. The second floor was never part of the theater and was occupied by various businesses during the Uptown's tenure.

At some point, he moved the concession stand inside the theater to boost his concession revenue. Prior to that renovation, the concession stand was next door, so getting another bag of popcorn meant going outside to the shop nearby. At first, his parents, Frank and Anna Barrett, ran the concession stand.

Concessions, he knew, were huge moneymakers, and in his contract with Commonwealth, he made sure to get a sweet deal for himself. His contract called for him to keep 25 percent of the concession's earnings as well as the typical deal of keeping 25 percent of the theater's ticket revenues.

Rex P. Barrett also made sure the theater would bring the crowds in even during Missouri's hot summers.

The process to keep it cool before the installation of air conditioning is legendary. A three-foot-by-five-foot block of ice was slid into a grate in the sidewalk in front of the movie theater, explained S Barre Barrett. A big fan pulled the air over the ice and blew it through the theater, making the Uptown "air cooled." Eventually, air conditioning was installed.

But the most important thing the Uptown had was Barrett, a man dedicated to three things: promotion, promotion and promotion.

## A TRULY GRAND OPENING

Those promotional efforts began with its grand opening, nearly as big and splashy as the Missouri's in 1928, far outstripping that for the Varsity in 1927.

Frank and Anna Barrett, Rex P. Barrett's parents, in the Uptown concession shop next door, before it was inside the theater. *Collection of S Barre Barrett.*

The Uptown's coverage filled almost the entire front page of the *Columbia Missourian* on May 18, 1935.

A headline in all capital letters stretched across the entire top of the front page, proclaiming, "UPTOWN THEATER OPENS DOORS TONIGHT."[94] The coverage highlighted the Commonwealth business model and included fourteen different articles about the new theater, including an outline of the first week's events.

An article highlighting the new, soft seats began by quoting the American Seating Company: "America has become 'soft-seat-conscious.'" It declared that when people ride on "soft automobile cushions, they don't want to sit on hard benches for the show," demonstrating the shift to driving to the movies and commenting on the once common bench seating in theaters.[95]

Another article described the "girl attaches…Miss Ruth Raneous, ticket seller, and the Misses Martha Whitaker and Mabel McGinnis, ushers," who were pictured in uniforms consisting of a light shirt with a bow at the collar and slacks.[96]

The décor was described as "modernistic simplicity." The front curtain on the stage was blue silk, the drapes in the foyer were blue velvet and the interior was "clothed in silk velvet and gold satin draperies," giving the impression of a room "that is inviting with a soft and colorful atmosphere."[97]

The Uptown décor shifted Columbia's movie theaters away from the lush movie palaces, but not to the the stripped-down box-like theaters that came later with their focus on convenience, location or the size of the screen.

## PROMOTION FOCUS OF KICK-OFF

Instead of glamour, the Uptown kickoff touted comfort and promotions, lots of promotions, to get people to come to the theater and keep them coming, heading off the already slipping movie admissions. The dip in movie attendance could be attributed to the fact that Prohibition ended in 1933 and people now had more options for nighttime entertainment. In addition, the country was still dealing with the Great Depression.

That meant movies had to offer something more and that something more was comfort and promotions.

To highlight comfort, one article promoting the grand opening outlined the use of natural gas for an "even temperature," while another noted the theater's use of "Western Electric Wide Range Sound" for a better and more realistic sound system. The headline read "Perfected Sound Ends Distortion."[98]

Opening night also included an outdoor program with Hawaiian dancers, the Hickman High School band and the American Legion Junior Drum and Bugle Corps. The opening event also featured appearances of out-of-town celebrities. The district managers of MGM Film Company, RKO Radio Pictures, Fox Film Company and the New York City manager of Warner Bros. were among those slated to attend the opening.

Finally, the Uptown opening included a promotion with an announcement of upcoming weekly amateur night contests at the Uptown for people to display any talent, from singing to playing a musical instrument, impersonations or "any entertainment specialty which will lend itself to radio presentation."

The contests would be broadcast on KFRU, and winners would go to a district-wide competition. The district winners would go on to an amateur night program to be aired on WDAF from a Kansas City theater stage.

Oh, and the movie program included two feature comedies, a cartoon and RKO-Pathé News.

The cost was ten cents cheaper than opening night at the Missouri Theatre, at twenty-five cents for adults and ten cents for children. The schedule was three shows daily—3:00, 7:00 and 9:00 p.m.—while on Saturday and Sunday the program was continuous from 1:00 to 11:00 p.m.

## NEVER-ENDING PUSH

The push to promote movie attendance at the Uptown and other Commonwealth movie theaters never ended while Rex P. Barrett was at the helm, and he had endless ingenious ideas along the way.

Some events were expected at that time, such as celebrity appearances. Pettit recalled the famous 1934 Dionne quintuplets making an appearance. Pettit said Barrett also used what today is called cross marketing, such as giving children free admittance with a few bread wrappers from a certain manufacturer.

Nichols, who worked with Barrett in the 1940s and 1950s, recalled when the Frankenstein movie was shown at the Uptown: at the end, an Uptown employee dressed up as Frankenstein's monster jumped off the stage, ran through the auditorium and picked up the cashier as a stunt.

Other events included baby pageants, pet shows, anything to get people into the theater. Ewing recalled going on a KFRU radio program sponsored by the theater that featured the top songs of the time. His job was to talk about a current or upcoming movie between each song. The Uptown also treated the entire University of Missouri football team to a free movie every Sunday night.

Even if the theater gave away the movie tickets, Barrett knew he was making money on the concessions.

## RACISM UNRAVELING

When the Uptown opened without an upstairs balcony, there was nowhere for the theater to segregate Black patrons like Columbia's other movie theaters did. Instead, Black customers weren't admitted, nor had they ever been admitted to the theater at that location, from when it opened as the Nickel in 1904 and throughout its name and ownership changes.

But in 1948, things were beginning to change. The Columbia chapter of CORE, Congress of Racial Equality, was organized, according to an article in the January/February issue of *Missouri Life* magazine, and was pushing for desegregation.[99]

In November 1953, thirty members of the group "tested" the Uptown to see if it "actually rejected Negros as customers." Robert Spencer, then manager of the Columbia's Commonwealth Theaters, said the members who approached the ticket booth and tried to buy tickets were told the theater was full and he then closed the theater's box office for the night.[100]

The movie showing was *Martin Luther*, a film about the 1500s church reformer. "Negro ministers" and members of a ministerial alliance had been invited to the see the movie, said Spencer, and he'd offered to schedule a special showing of the movie for "Negroes who wished to see the show." But, he said, the ministers told him that "they did not believe their people would be interested." The article noted the Uptown had always been segregated but added at the Boone on Eighth Street, "Negroes are permitted to occupy the entire balcony."[101]

By this time, Rex P. Barrett was the manager of all of Commonwealth's Columbia theaters and S Barre Barrett was working for his father at the time at the Hall. His father told him to let people sit anywhere they wanted to despite the Hall's policy to segregate Black patrons in the balcony. As S Barre Barrett explained, "He [his father] was OK with desegregation, but he didn't want to be at the forefront."

Less than a year later, the question would be moot. In May 1954, the U.S. Supreme Court ruled racial segregation was unconstitutional, and Columbia slowly desegregated its schools, restaurants and theaters.

## A HIDDEN PROBLEM

As a theater owner, Rex P. Barrett had an uncanny knack for promotion, but he also was a complicated man.

He was a World War I veteran, served two terms as Columbia's mayor (1937–39 and 1940–43), served as a colonel in the Missouri State Guard during World War II and was a husband and the father of four.

Rex P. Barrett, between his two terms as Columbia mayor, holds sons J. Larre (*left*) and Barre Barrett, 1943. *Collection of S Barre Barrett.*

But he struggled with the disease of alcoholism, and the illness stalked him for years.

Nichols recalled his days working for him during the 1940s and 1950s and said he was a peach of a guy, but he could be a tough cookie if he didn't like you. Rex P. Barrett could also be unpredictable. As several people put it, Rex P. Barrett was great—when he came to work. Yet before his illness took over, Rex P. Barrett was a mover and a shaker, exactly the kind of person he described in his 1934 dissertation as necessary for success in the movie theater industry.

And he was successful for years, opening the Boone Theatre with the same 25 percent ownership as the Uptown, said S Barre Barrett. He would go on to help open Columbia's first drive-in, the Broadway Drive-In, serving as Commonwealth's division manager and adding several theaters in Arkansas to the Commonwealth chain. He would go on to overseeing the Missouri, Hall and Varsity after Commonwealth took them over and again, manage to garner a quarter ownership there, too, before his retirement in 1961.

Rex P. Barrett's illness worsened as he grew older, and he died at sixty-nine, only four years after his retirement at sixty-five, a retirement marked by Commonwealth. The company lauded him with praise in its national newsletter, but the retirement may have been forced.

## CLOSED IN 1986: DEATH BY MULTIPLEXES

The Uptown, like all the downtown movie theaters, died from a series of challenges that drained moviegoers from the downtown theaters: television, suburbs, drive-ins and finally shopping center theaters and multiplexes. In February 1986, Commonwealth opened the Columbia Mall 4 and closed the Uptown. The building was bought by local businessmen who renovated it, removed the addition on the back that once housed the theater screen and stage and then returned it to its early purpose: retail space. Instead of selling hats, as of 2021, it housed a store that sold CDs, DVDs, Blu-ray and video games.

The Uptown Theatre in 1978. *Collections of the State Historical Society of Missouri.*

# 13

# THE BOONE, 1939-1955

## A BELOVED B-MOVIE VENUE

**N**o one loved the Boone Theatre as much as Nichols, who would go on to work in movie theaters for more than six decades, going from popcorn boy to projectionist to sound and projection expert.

His memories of the 1939 theater at 15 North Eighth Street recall a time when kids ran free and people went to the movies every week to see what happened to Flash Gordon, Buck Rogers or Dick Tracy.

Naturally, Nichols loved the Boone—he practically grew up in the 450-seat theater—and even got his first job there making popcorn at thirteen or fourteen years old.

"I was taken to the Boone when I was eight or so by a babysitter," said Nichols, who was born in 1931 and shared his memory at age eighty-nine in a 2020 telephone interview. "I'd go to the Boone at 10:00 a.m., watch right up until 7:00 p.m., when I'd go to the Varsity [just around the corner] for vaudeville."

Nichols recalled seeing the 1940 science fiction serial *Flash Gordon Conquers the Universe* at the theater at 15 North Eighth Street, as well as movies featuring Gene Autry, Roy Rogers and "Boston Blackie," the reformed jewel thief turned detective. Movie series like these kept patrons returning week after week to find out what happened to their favorite character and gave rise to terms like *cliff-hangers* and *sidekicks*.

These series were the bread and butter of the Boone, which was always a B-movie venue, as opposed to the Uptown, Commonwealth's first-run movie theater, or the College Theatre chain's theaters, the Hall and the

The Boone Theatre was built by Rex P. Barrett and Commonwealth Theaters in 1939. *Collection of S Barre Barrett.*

Missouri. When television came along with its own weekly program series, serial movies died out and so did the Boone. It closed in 1955 and was demolished in 1986.

## POPCORN BOY TO PROJECTIONIST

When Nichols became the popcorn boy, the concession stand was outside the theater, and even after it was moved inside the building, he said it never offered more than popcorn.

He got his big break one night when he was about fifteen and the projectionist didn't show up for work. Nichols had been hanging around the projectionist's booth, where he'd learn to run the movies, no easy feat back then.

At that time, the film was nitrate, so flammable that projectionist's booths had safety mechanisms that closed the room's window automatically if a fire began, sealing the projectionist inside but keeping the moviegoers safe.

"You didn't dare leave the booth because of the nitrate," recalled Nichols. The movies came in fifteen-to-eighteen-minute reels, and a projectionist had to switch reels to keep the movie going uninterrupted. So, for a fifty-five-

or sixty-two-minute B Western, a projectionist had to switch between two projectors several times to run the movie uninterrupted.

His job at the Boone led Nichols to a career that lasted about six decades. "I loved what I did, and I did it well," he said.

## CHEAP TICKETS, GOOD LOCATION

The Boone was Columbia's bargain movie theater. Built and owned by Barrett and Commonwealth Theaters, it was a cheaper movie house than the Uptown.

The Boone charged ten cents for children and fifteen cents for adults, and movies ran continuously from 1:00 p.m. to 11:00 p.m.

Commonwealth's other movie house, the Uptown, charged twenty-five cents for adults before 6:00 p.m. and thirty-five cents afterward, as did two of the College Theatre movie houses, Hall and Missouri. That chain's other movie theater, the Varsity, also charged fifteen cents for adults, but the movies there didn't run continuously.

Another way to save money on movie tickets was to redeem bread wrappers or milk bottles. Columbia native Barbra Horrell said as a girl she collected Pan-Dandy bread wrappers to get into the movies, while Nichols said he collected milk bottles to pay for admission.

The Boone's Eighth Street location also brought the movies closer to the Black residents of Columbia. It was two streets from the Sharp End, Columbia's Black business district, which ran from North Sixth to Fifth and Walnut to Ash, and its surrounding neighborhoods.

The Boone welcomed Black moviegoers, in contrast to the other Commonwealth theater, the Uptown, which, as mentioned, barred Black people from attending movies there. Nor did the Boone make Black patrons use a different entrance like the Missouri and the Hall did. Horrell said the Boone wasn't a luxury location and had less comfortable seating in the balcony, but she couldn't see movies at any of the theaters that made Black people use another entrance. Her parents forbid her from patronizing any business that required Black customers to use a side or back entrance.

But when civil rights improvements wiped out these restrictions, the Boone's lack of amenities became more apparent and may have led to the theater's 1955 closure. As noted, in 1953, Columbia civil rights groups began pushing for equal access in movie theaters and the 1954 U.S. Supreme Court ruling in *Brown vs. Board of Education* declared separate facilities were unconstitutional.

The Commonwealth chain may have simply had too many movie seats downtown. By 1955, the chain was operating the Missouri, Hall and Varsity and facing the problems of television driving down movie attendance.

Perhaps once Black patrons could go to any movie theater and everyone began to watch movies at home, the Boone's lack of luxury doomed it. The building was demolished in 1986.

But for Nichols, during an interview only months before his death in December 2020, the Boone Theatre remained bright in his memory.

# TIGER THEATRE, 1949–1960s

## COLUMBIA'S ONLY BLACK-OWNED MOVIE THEATER

C olumbia's only Black-owned movie theater, the Tiger Theatre,
opened in 1949 and closed as a theater in 1961, a victim of racism
and urban renewal.

From 1949 until 1961, the movie theater operated under several names,
starting out as the Frances.[102] From 1950 to 1958, it was called the Tiger
Theatre or the Tiger Arts Theatre. From 1959 to 1961, it was advertised as
the Princess Pam Art Theatre or just the Princess Pam.

It was demolished in 1986. Alvan B. Coleman and Edward "Dick" and
Ellis Tibbs," prominent Black businessmen who built the venue, sold it when
Columbia's Black business area, Sharp End, was cleared for urban renewal
in the 1960s.

In 1971, the building at 109 North Fifth Street was owned by Henry
"Hank" Waters. Then the owner of the nearby *Columbia Daily Tribune*
leased it to the Olde Un Theatre, Columbia's oldest operating adult movie
theater. Waters later razed the building to make room for the newspaper's
publishing plant.

### NO NEW RELEASES

From the beginning, the building did double and sometimes triple duty.
Built with a wall down the middle, creating two facilities, one side operated
as a convenience and liquor store while the other housed a restaurant and

The Tiger Theatre, 1961, was Columbia's only Black-built and Black-owned movie theater and operated under several names. *Collections of the State Historical Society of Missouri.*

operated as a theater in the early evening, switching to a nightclub after the movies ended.

But the theater never showed the newest releases.

In 1949, for example, it showed a 1947 flick, *Seven Were Saved*, and a 1946 Western, *Driftin' River*. At that time, it may have only showed movies on Fridays and Saturdays as well. In 1953, the Tiger was showing "second-run films and first-run 'art' movies."[103]

Racism was the reason behind the lack of first-run movies, said James Whitt, coordinator of Columbia's supplier diversity program and the chairman of Columbia's African-American Heritage Trail Committee. The committee is marking the history of Sharp End, a demolished Black business community.

"Black theaters were not on the distribution lists to get the latest movie," he explained. "That's a reality, a historic reality."

## RACISM: MOTHER OF INNOVATION

While Columbia's theaters had long served as more than movie venues, hosting Sunday school, high school graduations and political speakers, no other Columbia theaters featured multiple functions like the Tiger, with retail, movies and a nightclub operating in the same space. But this kind of variety was typical in Black communities, said Whitt, again pointing to racism as the cause. These multiuse buildings highlight the ingenuity, resilience and innovation of Black communities. He noted in his own childhood in Wayne, Indiana, one of his relatives owned a skating rink that doubled as a bowling alley and functioned as a lounge on weekends.

"When you don't have the resources, you make the best use of what you do have," said Whitt. "In the Black community, we got by with what we had." Black communities always pushed for equality and change, he said, but also had to deal with the reality of the time.

## COMMUNITY UPSTAGES BLOCKBUSTERS

In some ways, going to the movies at the Tiger wasn't about the movie itself.

The Tiger was in the Sharp End, the core of Columbia's Black community. Roughly, it included much of Walnut to Ash Streets between Fifth and Sixth Streets. As the Black business district, it was filled with a wide variety of businesses surrounded by the Black community, neighborhoods and churches. This area offered a safe harbor where Black people could feel safe and experience community without many of the restrictions of White society and racism.

As Horrell, who grew up nearby, explained, "We grew up separate but equal. We couldn't care less what happened outside the First Ward. We were fine."

She recalled going to the movies at the one-story Tiger, explaining, "We didn't think about what movies were showing." It was enough that it was their neighborhood movie theater and Black patrons didn't have to endure the humiliation of using a different entrance or sitting in the balcony. Horrell said the Tiger did show some first-run movies but also a lot of Black movies.

But history marched on. As noted, in 1954 segregation was declared unconstitutional.

## OPENING UP AND CLOSING DOWN

Other cultural changes affected the Tiger. As automobile transportation took over, the Tiger began to advertise its free parking.

Then, in 1959, the Tiger changed its name to the Princess Pam and became an art film theater, offering movies that pushed the limits of the movie codes, and called itself "Columbia's Only Art Theatre." It was showing the 1954 movie *The Time of Desire*, a Swedish film that had premiered in the United States in 1958. The ad included an image of two young girls and stated, "Call it Passion…Love or Sin! With girls so young what strange dreams may come alive at the touch of first love."[104] Other movies shown in 1959 included the 1956 *Street of Shame*, a Japanese film about prostitutes, followed by a 1953 comedy and then the steamy *Tides of Passion* from 1956.

After 1961, the ads for the Princess Pam seem to disappear, so perhaps the niche for art house movies was taken over in 1967 when Commonwealth reopened the Varsity as the Film Arts Theatre, which operated until 1972.

By the 1960s, the Tiger/Princess Pam was also facing the results of the Land Clearance and Redevelopment Authority's urban renewal plan. It had cleared away many of the Sharp End's businesses as well as nearby housing, leaving a few buildings and fewer customers for places like the Princess Pam.

## COLEMAN AND TIBBS: ENTREPRENEURS

But until the area was cleared, it was filled with entrepreneurs like Coleman and Tibbs.

In 1949, the Sharp End area was thriving and the nearby Boone Theatre on Eighth Street was doing a booming business, but it confined Black patrons to the balcony. Coleman and Tibbs may have wanted to free Black people from that restriction—or they might have seen an opportunity to cash in on the movie industry.

Alvan B. Coleman's father, James Boyd Coleman, was the principal of Douglass School in 1909, while he and his wife ran Coleman's Hand Laundry, and both were teachers. He passed that drive for education and his entrepreneurial spirit on. His son Alvan B. Coleman was a college graduate, and from 1940 to 1960, the younger Coleman owned and operated Central Marketing Co., Scott's Taxi, Green Tree Tavern, Coleman Coal and Salvage, the Tiger Lounge and South Town Liquors, the South Town Variety Store and several apartments.[105]

Alvan B. Coleman teamed up with Ed Grant "Dick" Tibbs, a Columbia native. Like Coleman, he was an entrepreneur. In addition to the Tiger, Tibbs owned and operated a long list of businesses, including the Kingfish Smoke Shop and Shoe Shining, T&T Smoke Shop, the Deluxe Billiards

& Pool Hall, Central Marketing and Green Tree Tavern.[106] His business interests included the Paradise Club, and he owned residential and business properties as well.[107]

Tibbs's son Ed Tibbs lauded his father's business acumen: "I think he had a sixth-grade education....He was a smart man. He didn't have a degree but he had a PhD in business. To have what he had in those days...to keep it and be able to pass it on the way he did, it took some intelligence."[108]

One of the properties he passed on is near where the Tiger once was, and it is now owned by Ed Tibbs. The Tibbs building at Fifth and Walnut has housed Tony's Pizza Palace for decades. The building is also now marked as a historic site on the African-American Heritage Trail, as is the Tiger Theatre location.

The Tiger Theatre building may be gone, but its history—and its example to entrepreneurs—remains.

# 15

# BROADWAY DRIVE-IN THEATRE, 1949–1973

## COLUMBIA'S FIRST DRIVE-IN

**M**onkeys. Ponies. A playground. Oh, my! And movies and color cartoons! These attractions and more were on tap at the Broadway Drive-In, Columbia's first drive-in movie theater. It opened on June 11, 1949, and closed in 1973.

The ad for opening night at the 530-car outdoor theater spells out the allures of seeing a movie under the stars:

> *Smoke when you like! Come as you are! Don't worry about clothes! Individual Speakers! Adjust your own volume! Perfect visibility from any part of the theatre! Complete privacy! Your neighbors won't bother you! Finest refreshments! Health-Conditioned by nature…enjoy cool breezes under the stars! Playground for the kiddies—let the kids have fun! Children under 12 admitted free![109]*

Wearing what you like acknowledged that at the time, people dressed up to go to the movies, but now, America was going casual, one car at a time.

The Broadway Drive-In was built by Rex P. Barrett and Commonwealth. Bob Walter was the first manager of the roughly $150,000 operation.[110]

Columbia's first drive-in was part of a boom in drive-ins across the nation. The trend stemmed from America's love affair with the car as well as the baby boom underway following the return of servicemen from World War II. Drive-ins benefited from the availability of cheap land and moviegoers moving to suburbia.

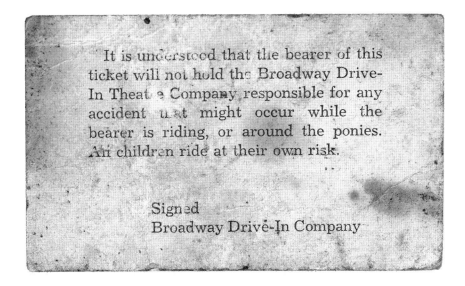

It is understood that the bearer of this ticket will not hold the Broadway Drive-In Theat e Company responsible for any accident u t might occur while the bearer is riding, or around the ponies. An children ride at their own risk.

Signed
Broadway Drive-In Company

The 530-car Broadway Drive-In featured pony rides and a playground. It opened in 1949 and closed in 1973. *Collections of the Boone County Historical Society.*

The Broadway Drive-In Theatre operated at 1729 Broadway, now the Broadway Shopping Center. *Collections of the State Historical Society of Missouri.*

When the Broadway was under construction, a photograph of a sign announcing the coming theater shows fences and a pasture with the screen rising out of an open field. The theater's first address in city directories and telephone books was simply West Broadway, no address number. The screen faced Broadway and Clinkscales at an angle on Ash Street, which was a gravel road then.

## A SHORT RIDE

Drive-ins had a short burst of popularity. The first drive-in opened in 1933 in Camden, New Jersey, but then construction of outdoor theaters slowed during World War II due various shortages. By 1949, there were 1,000 drive-ins across the country, up from 103 in 1946. By 1955, there would be more than 4,000 drive-ins.

But by 1986, when the Sky-Hi, Columbia's third and last movie theater, closed, there were about only 2,000 drive-ins across the nation. By 2020, there were only 321 drive-ins left, according to the National Association of Theatre Owners.

The Broadway's 1973 closure was blamed on the continuing slide in movie attendance and the encroaching housing that meant nearby homes could easily see what was being shown on the screen. This meant the Broadway had to confine its movies to those with G or PG ratings, but by then, drive-in audiences had shifted to young adults who wanted to see R-rated, horror or science fiction films, not just Walt Disney and family flicks.

At the same time, land prices were increasing, which meant a lot big enough to park 530 cars was pricey.

Two other trends hurt drive-ins. The move toward smaller cars meant a drive-in wasn't as comfortable as before, and the movie theater industry was moving toward multiplexes. In the early 1970s, Commonwealth opened Columbia's first multiplex, the Campus Twin, and two other multiplexes were opened by other theater companies: the Biscayne 3 Cinemas in 1972 and White Gate Twin in 1973.

Drive-in consumers wanted better screens and sound systems, and many movie theater owners either couldn't or wouldn't upgrade the old movie theaters in the face of falling revenues. Finally, consumers wanted more creature comforts, including freedom from creatures like mosquitos and Missouri's weather. By the late 1960s, most homes were being built with air conditioning, and fewer people were willing to swelter as they watched a movie.

## WHAT DO MOVIES HAVE TO DO WITH IT?

Almost immediately, drive-ins had trouble getting blockbusters because the movie studios resisted renting their best material to them. But just as quickly, drive-in theater operators realized the movies didn't matter.

The Broadway Drive-In's opening night movie was a year old. The draw to the drive-in was freedom to smoke or drink or just relax in your own car. Later, in the 1960s, the same kids who scampered around the playground would return to the drive-in for the freedom from adult supervision, until they migrated to shopping centers and malls.

As the years went by, the lag between the release of a movie and it showing at the drive-in grew until eventually the movies at drive-ins could be years old.

But while they lasted, the drive-ins were moneymakers for theater owners. Drive-ins were cheaper to build than indoor movie theaters and returned more money on concessions than traditional movie theaters.

In 1952, concessions at drive-ins earned forty-five cents for every dollar spent at the ticket booth compared to twenty-six cents earned at an indoor theater concession stand, according to Kerry Segrave in *Drive-In Theaters*.[111]

Those numbers explain why drive-in employee Tom R. Shrout Jr.'s only regret about working at the drive-ins as a teenager was how harsh he was when someone tried to sneak in "hidden" moviegoers—most obvious when "a person would drive up to the ticket booth with one person in the car." He realized later stowaway moviegoers didn't matter to the theater's bottom line. "If you could get them to buy a hot dog, popcorn and a coke, you were even," he said.

Drive-ins were a bargain to build, too. Cost comparisons from 1952 cited in *Drive-In Theaters* show construction costs for an indoor movie theater were $243 per seat, while for a drive-in the cost was calculated at $73 per seat.[112]

This cost differential endured. In 1966, Commonwealth opened the Cinema, an 850-seat indoor theater, and the Sky-Hi Drive-In for 750 cars in 1965. The construction costs equaled $264.71 per indoor seat versus $86.42 per drive-in seat, assuming a 2.7 person per vehicle calculation.

The economic downside for outdoor movie theaters was the shorter season, but in Columbia, the drive-ins typically opened in February or March and closed in October or November, leaving them shuttered for only a few months.

Some things were the same for a drive-in or an indoor theater: the need for promotion.

Nichols, who worked at the Broadway, recalled a "chicken toss," where they threw live chickens off the concession stand at the Broadway to the crowds. Another promotion was challenging people to find an actual needle in a haystack as well as a snake exhibit. Some promotions even made money for the drive-in during the day. One promotion Nichols recalled involved a man in a casket buried alive for a week. "During the day we charged for them to see the guy buried," Nichols said. "We had big crowds for that."

Another similarity between the indoor and outdoor movie theaters was the sense of connection among the workers at the drive-ins, often young people in high school who would be recruited by one of their school chums or were the children of the owners and managers. If you couldn't make your shift, you simply called someone else you knew who worked for the theaters and asked her or him to come in for you, said Debbie Richerson, the daughter of Walter, the Broadway's first manager. Later, as business increased in the 1970s, a more formal system developed with interviews and references, she added.

"It was a good young-person-going-to-work experience," said Shrout Jr., even though his mother wasn't thrilled about him working at the drive-in because he'd get home late after the movies. But sometimes the real reason he got home late is because he would hang out at the theater playing cards in the back room with his friends from work, only to get home at 6:00 a.m.

But eventually ponies and playgrounds couldn't save the Broadway from closure.

When Commonwealth closed the Broadway in 1973 to build more retail space at the Broadway Shopping Center, Columbia was left with one drive-in, the Sky-Hi on Old Highway 63—and its opening night ad didn't tout its playground.

# 16

# PARKADE DRIVE-IN THEATRE, 1953–1961

## AN UNUSUAL CONCESSION STAND

Today, the Parkade Plaza stands where Nipper the pony once roamed and Judy Jeans Glaister lived as a little girl at the Parkade Drive-In Theatre.

Glaister isn't nostalgic about the three or four years she lived at the drive-in, and you can't blame her. "It was lonely," she said. "I didn't live in a neighborhood with people, and I had to walk home alone," recalled Glaister, who was ten years old at the time.

Her father, Herb Jeans, built the Parkade Drive-In Theatre in 1953 with a unique design—Glaister's home, the family apartment, was above the concession stand. The T-shaped building stood in the middle of the four-hundred-car drive-in parking lot.

So, while her pals walked home and played in the streets together, she looked out at rows of the pickets that held the car speakers.

The drive-in's unusual design earned it two full pages in a national publication of the movie theater industry.[113]

Its unusual design isn't the Parkade's only claim to fame. Jeans closed it in 1961 and demolished it to build mid-Missouri's first enclosed shopping center.

Glaister admits there were upsides to living at the drive-in. She and her sister, the late Dorcas Sue Jeans Miller Holden, got to see all the movies with sound provided by a speaker in the apartment. "We had a perfect view of the screen," said Glaister, because the second story also housed the projector as well as her father's office.

*Above*: The Parkade Drive-In Theatre opened in 1953 where Parkade Plaza is today. *Collection of Judy Jeans Glaister.*

*Opposite, top*: Judy Jeans Glaister is shown in the apartment where she and her family lived above the Parkade's concession stand. *Collection of Judy Jeans Glaister.*

*Opposite, bottom*: The Parkade concession stand featured an apartment, the projector and office on the second floor. *Collection of Judy Jeans Glaister.*

She also got to ride the Parkade pony, Nipper, who she doesn't recall living up to his name, as well as the pony at the Broadway Drive-In, as part of her childhood chores. Glaister also worked in the concession stand and helped in the ticket booth, which she enjoyed. "You got to see your friends," she recalled.

Her father supervised the construction of the drive-in himself and broke ground less than a year before the Parkade's opening on March 27, 1953. It cost $90,000, including $15,000 for the projector, only $20,000 more than the $125,000 price tag for the one-hundred-car-larger Broadway Drive-In Theatre built in 1949. The cost of the Parkade would equal $889,896.99 in 2021 dollars.

On-site apartments were common at drive-ins but were typically in the screen tower.[114] The Parkade, Glaister said, also had an apartment in its screen tower, but the theater's caretaker lived there. She and her family lived in the apartment for three or four years until they moved into a house in the Highridge subdivision, which her father developed.

Designing the building was challenge, and the result was innovative. Since the apartment housed the projection booth, the architect had to make sure the lights from the apartment wouldn't shine onto the movie screen. To solve this problem, the design included a special roof overhang and "awning-type windows."[115]

## COLUMBIA'S FIRST MALL

In 1961, when Jeans decided to build Columbia's first mall, initially he struggled to get financial backing. His daughter said since the concept was new to Columbia, people weren't sure it would work.

Parkade Plaza opened in 1965 with anchor stores J.C. Penney, Kroger, the Flaming Pit restaurant and Missouri's largest Ben Franklin five-and-dime store, according to newspaper accounts at the time. After the Columbia Mall opened in 1985 and the city grew, many of the original stores and restaurants moved out of the Parkade, but it remains an active space with a mix of retail, restaurants and office space.

Herb Jeans closed the drive-in to build the Parkade Plaza. Jeans served as Columbia mayor from 1969 to 1971. *Collection of Judy Jeans Glaister.*

Later, as the popularity of drive-ins faded, such conversions to shopping centers were common. Yet Glaister wasn't surprised her father took on the challenge before everyone else. "He was determined, and he persevered and made it," she said.

Jeans had a history of trying new occupations. The family moved to Warsaw, Missouri, where he operated the Roxy, an indoor movie theater, after teaching seventh and eighth grades in rural Montgomery County for seven years. After opening the Parkade Drive-In, Jeans developed the Lee Del Trailer Court, also on the drive-in site, and the Rainbow Trailer Court.[116]

In 1967, Jeans ran for mayor and lost. He then redoubled his efforts and won in 1969 by three thousand votes and served from 1969 to 1971.[117] Explaining his eventual victory, he said, "You can do almost anything you want to if you're willing to put the time, effort and brains into it."[118]

During Jeans's time as mayor, Columbia passed a one-cent city sales tax by a 6–4 margin, and he favored the development of neighborhood "pocket parks," as well as bringing light industry to Columbia. He didn't seek reelection in 1971, stating he wanted to spend time with his family and on his business. He sold the Parkade Plaza in 1973 and died in 1975 at sixty-three.[119]

While the concession stand and apartment combination was unusual, the focus of the Parkade was the same as all drive-in theaters at the time—amenities along with some movies. The playground included a merry-go-round, slides, swings and a picnic area. The festivities in 1953 on opening night included fireworks, a clown act and gifts. The ad, almost as an afterthought, included the name of the movie, *Flame of Araby*, in Technicolor—a 1951 film.[120]

Continued promotions remained the key to drive-in operations. A March 6, 1959 ad offered, "Free gasoline for your car heater. One gallon of gas free to each car if the temperature drops below 40 degrees so that you may watch the show in comfort." The movie was *Thunder Road* with Robert Mitchum—only a year old—and the ad included the usual tagline, "Come as you are. Bring the Kiddies!"[121]

And Glaister? She didn't go into the movie industry business. After graduating from Stephens College, she went into nursing education, traveled the world and developed a private practice as a therapist, finally settling in Galveston, Texas.

As for her memories of living at the drive-in, "It had its fun times."

# SKY-HI DRIVE-IN THEATRE, 1965–1986

## LOOKING FOR DARK SKIES

Timing is everything, and in 1965, when Commonwealth opened the Sky-Hi Drive-In Theatre, society was changing.

As noted, drive-in numbers were dropping. From 1955 to 1965, they had fallen from roughly 4,000 to less than 3,500. By the time the 700-car Sky-Hi closed in 1986, little more than half of those drive-ins remained, with only 321 drive-ins left as of 2020.

Along with the drop in drive-in theaters, movie admissions were going down. By 1965, only a tenth of the U.S. population went to the movies weekly.

But the Broadway Drive-In was being engulfed by the city and the lighting that comes with housing. Commonwealth opened the Sky-Hi Drive-In Theatre on what was then "outside of town," at 3110 Old 63 South, and in a bowl-like area.

On opening night, like Columbia's other two other drive-ins, its ads lauded its amenities and included plenty of promotion with a mere mention of the movie. When it opened, the Sky-Hi's claim to fame was that it had "the largest air-conditioned snack bar in Central Missouri."[122] Later, its two-line cafeteria with pizza on the menu would be lauded as well.[123]

The opening night movies were *Quick Before It Melts* (1964) and the Henry Fonda movie *The Rounders* (1965). As usual, opening festivities included plenty of pizazz, with rockets, prizes and even a "Sky-Hi Disc-A-Go-Go Girl" dancing on the roof of the concession stand.

In case moviegoers planned on watching the movie, the theater did provide a good setting away from the light pollution of the city, clear visibility and sound. The screen stood 20 feet off the ground, was 105 by 50 feet and cost $20,000; the parking area sloped downward, giving every parking spot a good view. The drive-in cost $175,000 to build and included "modern speakers and electric in-car heaters to make winter viewing comfortable."[124]

When it opened, manager Richard Ytell had said the theater would show family entertainment, but later, like other drive-ins, the Sky-Hi showed R-rated movies. By 1973, an April 27 ad included only R-rated movies, including *Sex Is a Woman*.[125]

In 1975, the first VCR hit the stores in the United States, and the nation's first video rental store opened in 1977. The country's first Blockbuster store opened in 1985, and soon people began to watch even more movies at home instead of heading out to the theater or the drive-in.

In 1986, Commonwealth closed the Sky-Hi, and as of 2021, the road is lined with apartment buildings. The only sign of the former drive-in is the Sky-Hi Storage at 2801 Old 63 South.

# PART V

# YOUR CHOICE: QUALITY, QUANTITY OR QUIRKY

# THE CINEMA THEATRE, 1966–1998

## COLUMBIA'S FIRST SHOPPING CENTER THEATER AND ITS BIGGEST SCREEN

B efore the Cinema Theatre went up in 1966, moviegoers had a choice between seeing a movie at a downtown movie theatre or a drive-in with meals, the freedom to smoke and enjoy the beverage of your choice and let the kids run.

But after Commonwealth Theaters built the Cinema, another option popped up with the focus on comfort, convenience and the movie, in just about that order.

From then on, movie theaters would basically be a box where people could sit in plush rocking or reclining chairs in a building they could walk to from a convenient parking lot to see their choice of a movie on a good screen.

It would be not until 1998 that the Ragtag Film Society would reclaim the pleasures of watching an intriguing movie and sharing that experience with a community where a plush environment wasn't the selling point.

The Cinema closed in 1998, a victim of the Commonwealth collapse and the ensuing musical chairs of Columbia movie theater owners with venues being bought, sold and resold and closed. The former Cinema now houses Upscale Resale, a store operated by a charity that sells used clothing and other items.

When it opened on June 8, 1966, the Cinema made history for three reasons.

First, it was Columbia's largest single-screen movie theatre. When it closed in 1998, it was Columbia's last single-screen movie theater.

Second, it was the first indoor movie theater built by Commonwealth in Columbia in thirty years, although during that time, in 1949, entrepreneurs Tibbs and Coleman had built the Tiger Theatre.

Third, it marked a short-lived shift in movie theaters toward movie theaters in shopping centers. It was the Commonwealth Theatres chain's first such shopping center theater house and opened in the Broadway Shopping Center. Soon, other companies would build movie theaters in shopping centers, including the original Forum Theatre in 1967 in the Forum Shopping Center and the Biscayne 3 Cinemas in 1972 in the Biscayne Shopping Center. In 1986, Commonwealth would build another shopping center theater, the Columbia Mall 4 at the Columbia Mall.

But the Cinema missed the trend that would spell its doom—the move toward multiplexes begun in 1963 in Kansas City by Stan Durwood of AMC with the Parkway Twin. The Cinema Theatre opened featuring one high-quality fifty-five-by-twenty-two-foot screen and 833 seats.

When it closed on November 29, 1998, after a thirty-two-year run, it was then owned by the Dallas-based Hollywood Theatre chain. Hollywood blamed its closure on film distributors' reluctance to send prints of new films to single-screen theaters.[126] However, the Hollywood chain had just opened its fourteen-screen multiplex, the Hollywood Theaters 14, on Stadium, and also closed its other Columbia theater, the downtown Campus Twin.

The Cinema came under Hollywood ownership in 1996, after Commonwealth sold it to United Artists Theatres in 1989, which then sold it to Crown Cinema in 1990.

## OPENS WITH THE GOVERNOR

Unlike the Sky-Hi Drive-In that had opened a year prior with local go-go dancers, the opening of the Cinema Theatre featured a speech by Governor Warren E. Hearnes. The grand opening also featured Miss Cinema, Donna Fogle, proclaimed as Columbia's Future Miss America, who welcomed each lady with a carnation.[127] Clearly Commonwealth was expecting a different kind of crowd at its newest Columbia crown jewel than those who would find go-go dancers appealing.

The opening night ad was stuffed with alluring details and exclamation marks, including, "The magic screen will blossom in this totally new theatre!" The other details included "luxurious American Recliner Seating, climate-controlled cooling and heating, Walker Super Hi-Lite Screen, latest in projection lens."[128]

It opened with the *Glass Bottom Boat* and, even before its opening, began touting its next draw, a four-week engagement for *The Sound of Music* with tickets sold on a reserve basis. The Cinema was planned to be a first-run movie theater.[129]

When Commonwealth was building the theater, it planned to name it the Crest, projected construction costs were $225,000 and it was to feature 850 seats.[130]

Instead, the theater opened with 833 seats—but what seats! A newspaper article described them at length, noting that 521 of the seats would be "rockers" and recline to a lounging position. "We think about audience comfort first," said Earl Douglass, Commonwealth district manager. All this, Commonwealth management noted, came at the same price as the other Columbia Commonwealth properties, $1.25 per ticket for adults, $0.50 for children.[131] By the way, that $1.25 ticket price translates into $10.30 in 2021 dollars.

The décor included an interior of gold, brown, pale green and yellow and carpeting with a "special Alexander Smith Hawaiian floral design.... Outside the theater, persons will enjoy another new concept in Columbia movie theaters—a footman and a parking lot attendant. The pressures of parking close to the theater will not be a problem, as space for 500 cars is available."[132]

Sadly, those amenities highlighted the lack of those conveniences at Commonwealth's downtown movie palace theaters with their one-thousand-plus seats, which led to their closures in the late 1980s. People were beginning to demand easy parking and multiplexes.

So, like the Cinema's footmen and parking lot attendants, the first shopping center movie theater came to an end, bowing to moviegoers' demands.

**19**

# THE FORUM, FORUM 8, 1967–PRESENT

## COLUMBIA'S SECOND SHOPPING CENTER THEATER

Opened in 1967, the original Forum was the last single-screen theater built in Columbia. It was replaced in 1992 by the Forum 8, built behind the shopping center, which was Columbia's largest multiplex until 1997, when the Hollywood built the Stadium 14.

Now it's a movie theater pandemic survivor. The Forum 8 reopened in September 2020 with reduced seating after the closures of the 2020–21 coronavirus pandemic.

But this eight-screen multiplex knows how to roll with the punches.

The original Forum Theatre was in the newly developed Forum Shopping Center, and its address was 1400 South West Boulevard. Today, that road is known as Forum Boulevard. The original Forum's grand entrance alluded to the ancient Roman forum theme of the Forum Shopping Center. The theater featured alcoves with statues on each side of the entrance that are still there, but now they flank the entrance to Postal & Sign Express, a shipping and packaging firm. The rest of the former movie theater space has since been converted to shops and office space.

The original Forum one-screen venue had 816 seats, and admission was $1.50 for adults and $0.50 for children, according to cinematreasures.org, a website devoted to movie theater information. The opening night movie was the World War II drama *Tobruk* with Rock Hudson.

Over the years, the shopping center was expanded, and the area where the Forum once operated now marks the corner of the shopping center.

The Forum 8, opened in 1992, replacing the one-screen Forum Theatre that operated in the Forum Shopping Center from 1967 to 1992. *Courtesy of Deanna Dikeman, May 2021.*

In June 1992, the Forum closed, and the Forum 8 opened at 1209 Forum Katy Parkway, as noted, behind the shopping center. The new theater was part of the movie theater trend toward multiplexes rather than single-screen venues.

The Forum 8's auditoriums ranged from 158 to 354 at pre-pandemic levels; as of May 2021, pandemic social distancing requirements meant the auditoriums ranged from 56 to 100 seats.

Over the years, the Forum and then the Forum 8 survived the challenges of the advent of video movie rentals in the late 1970s, the expansion of video rentals and later DVD rentals in retail stores and groceries in the 1990s and the shift to streaming led by Netflix in 2007.

Along the way, the Forum 8 also benefited from some changes in Columbia's movie theater industry such as the closing of many of Columbia's movie houses.

But in March 2021, Forum 8 manager Wes Halsey said the theater was losing money. During the pandemic, studios either didn't release top movies or released them directly to streaming services.[133]

Prior to the pandemic, movie studios would release a movie for theater-only distribution prior to releasing it to streaming services. During the pandemic, movie studios shortened or waived the movie theater exclusive time period. As the pandemic appeared to recede in spring of 2021, the movie theater industry remained in flux. Some movie theater chains have been negotiating for movie theater–only releases, and others are pushing for shortened movie theater–only releases. Some studios have shifted to releasing movies directly to streaming platforms.[134]

The Forum 8 has faced its own changes during the decades it has been open. Originally, it was owned by the Overland Park, Kansas–based Dickinson Theatres chain. Later, Goodrich Quality Theaters chain bought it but declared bankruptcy in February 2020. In July 2020, the Namdar Realty Group bought the Goodrich assets, including the theaters, and rebranded them GQT Movies. Namdar is a Great Neck, New York commercial real estate investment firm.

In September 2020, when it reopened, the Forum 8 reduced ticket prices to $6.25 for children and $7.75 for seniors, according to a *Columbia Daily Tribune* article on September 2, 2020.[135]

As of this writing, people are trickling back into the movie theater and the Forum 8 is popping corn and showing movies, just as it has for twenty-nine years at that location and fifty-four years since it opened its doors.

# 20

# THE OLDE UN THEATRES, 1971–PRESENT

## COLUMBIA'S ONLY WOMAN-RUN THEATER

Like all theater owners, Debbie Simon has faced plenty of challenges over the years from the economy and technology changes that allow people to see movies at home instead of in a movie theater.

But she faces obstacles other movie theater owners don't—like protestors and legislators trying to shut down her business and economic discrimination—because of the kind of business she runs, adult entertainment.

Simon owns the Olde Un Theatres, a three-screen theater and retail business she took over in the late 1980s from her father, Roger Snodgrass. Simon is the second woman in Columbia to operate a movie theater since Della Craigo, operated the Nickelodeon in 1907. She runs the business with the help of longtime manager, now assistant manager, Richard Simpson.

The Olde Un is also one of Columbia's longest-running movie theaters, operating since 1971. Only the Forum Theatre, which opened as a single-screen theater in 1967, preceded it. It opened under the ownership of Dave Grinpas, who later shifted to co-owner and moved to California. Snodgrass took over leading the Olde Un, and in 1986, it moved from its original location at 109 North Fifth Street to its current location, 101 East Walnut Street.

Finally, the Olde Un was the first adult theater in Columbia to open a gay-oriented theater. In 1976, the Olde Un opened a ten-to-twelve-seat screening room called the Cabaret.

The Olde Un Theatres moved to 101 East Walnut in 1986 from 109 North Fifth Street. *Courtesy of Ginny Booker, May 2021.*

## WHO GOES TO THE UN?

It seems the Olde Un is the theater everyone says they've never been to—but they have.

Simpson, who has worked at the Olde Un since 1971, said, "It's truly hard to find someone who hasn't been here."

Customers, said Simon, represent every walk of life and gender orientation, and these days include more and more women. She admits before the 2020–21 pandemic forced them to close their theaters, the majority of moviegoers were men. The Olde Un has three theaters with screens for seating ten, twenty and thirty.

Even before the pandemic, only one-fifth of the theater's revenues came from showing movies. The rest of the Olde Un's income comes from its retail area, where it sells items such as mugs, clothing, vibrators, DVDs and gag gifts. The Olde Un also has an online store and, as of 2021, employed eleven full- and part-time employees—a number down from the twenty-two to twenty-four people it employed before a 2010 Missouri law limited its hours. Prior to that legal change, the Olde Un was open twenty-four hours a day, allowing it to cash in on the after-the-bar-closed retail business. It's now open from 7:00 a.m. until midnight.

Other changes that have eaten into the Olde Un's revenue include online streaming and free online pornography sites.

But Simon and Snodgrass are used to rolling with the economic punches. The theater survived bomb scares in 1984, antipornography protests in 1986 as well as the advent of VCRs and DVDs.

It's also gotten boosts from unlikely sources like the celebrity Oprah, when her show featured the benefits of vibrators in 2009. That's the same year the *New York Times* covered the fact that sex toys had gone mainstream, and today, those items are on sale everywhere.

Simon acknowledged you can order online some of the items the Olde Un has on the shelves, but you can't look at them, touch them or ask questions, like you can at Olde Un. All the workers there have seen and heard everything. No question causes any one of them to blink an eye.

Simon, with a degree from the University of Missouri in fashion design, and Simpson's no-nonsense approach to the retail business make sure the store is women-friendly. About half of the staff are women, and the store is bright, light and filled with displays a lot like any mall store. Stepping inside, you're greeted by clothing that you can't find at most boutiques and shoes you won't want to wear to the grocery.

## WHO'S IN CHARGE?

Both Simon and Simpson are as far from any stereotype of an owner of an adult entertainment theater as you can get.

A bright blond, Simon, sixty-one, is quick with a laugh and keeps an eye on marketing and retail opportunities and is straightforward about describing Olde Un's products, movies and product and movie categories.

She's a family person, thrilled to talk about her stepdaughter and three grandchildren, along with a large extended family. "That's my favorite role. I love being a grandmother," said Simon.

As for Simpson, at seventy-one, he looks more like Santa Claus without the white beard than any outdated image of a porn theater manager. A family man, he's proud of his adult daughter and calls her the light of his life. His attitude toward his nearly five decades at the Olde Un is simple: It's about business. He compares the business to McDonald's and sums it up as providing good products, having a friendly staff and standing behind the products.

Richard Simpson, assistant manager, and Debbie Simon, owner of the Olde Un Theatres, Columbia's second woman-owned theater. *Collection of Richard Simpson.*

As he puts it, people can count on the Olde Un: "We've been a legitimate business for forty-nine years, making payroll every week, and we're going to be here tomorrow."

## HISTORY

The Olde Un got its start in 1971 and was the only adult entertainment venue between Kansas City and St. Louis, said Simpson. Roger Snodgrass had an adult bookstore on Ninth Street called Midwest Mercantile. Dave Grinpas opened the seventy-five-seat Olde Un Theatre and named it after an adult movie theater in Kansas City known as the Olde Chelsea, explained Simpson.

Simpson was attending the University of Missouri's School of Journalism studying photography, working construction in his spare time, when he helped Grinpas remodel the 109 North Fifth Street building. After the project was over, Grinpas offered him a job. Simpson had also worked at Commonwealth's Film Arts theater in the former Varsity, so he was familiar with projectors. He's been on the job ever since, except for two years when he toured with a band.

In 1973, Snodgrass moved his bookstore into half of the building and renamed it the Midwest Adult Bookstore. In the 1980s, Grinpas moved to San Diego, California, and Snodgrass and Simpson combined the two entities. At roughly the same time, Debbie Simon returned from a career in retail in California and began to manage the operation under the tutelage of Simpson.

In 1984, an antipornography group organized, and there were two bomb threats against the Olde Un and the *Columbia Daily Tribune*. The newspaper was targeted because the paper's owner Henry "Hank" J. Waters III owned the building and leased it to theater.

The bombs were duds, and warning calls to the police kept the scare to a minimum. Simpson said the theater didn't close.

In 1986, Snodgrass decided to bring nude dancing to the Olde Un as an attempt to replace falling revenues due to the encroaching home video players. Protestors picketed, and the group urged the city council to shut down the Olde Un. The council declined, citing the lack of legal support for closing down a legitimate business.

A few months later, Simpson said, the novelty of nude dancing wore off and the effort of booking and organizing the entertainment didn't balance its slight increase in revenue.

By then, Simon was on board, and she began the ever-increasing shift of the business to what she calls "joys and toys," retail items for every taste and preference—from X-rated macaroni to bachelorette items.

In 1999, the Olde Un underwent a $100,000 expansion.

Since the 2010 legislative change limiting the hours of adult entertainment venues, business at the Olde Un has been shifting continually toward retail and away from movie theater revenue.

Yet, Simon said, the theaters will also be there, and she sees their offerings as a need. Many people, she notes, are concerned about privacy and don't want to stream adult movies. For those folks, the Olde Un also offers DVDs, books and magazines.

For Simpson and Simon, it's just business. "We don't try to rile anyone up," said Simon. But she did wish her property insurance wouldn't get canceled every few years. Her agent tells her the companies just don't want to insure a business in the adult entertainment industry.

Just like the early movie theaters had to overcome concerns about fire safety, Simon and Simpson have faced bomb threats, protestors and changing technology.

The Olde Un isn't going anywhere because, as Simon puts it, "People like a hint of naughty."

# 21

# THE CAMPUS I & II, 1971–1997

## COLUMBIA'S FIRST MULTIPLEX

Today, you can buy a tent or outdoor clothing from the Alpine Shop, where moviegoers once watched movies at the Campus Twin Theatres I & II, Columbia's first multiplex theater.

Opened in 1971, it closed in November 1997 due to the opening of the fourteen-screen multiplex, the Hollywood Stadium 14, now the Regal Columbia & RPX. During its twenty-six years at Broadway and Hitt Street, it was called the Campus Cinema I & II, Campus I & II and the Campus Twin.

When the Campus Twin opened on September 8, 1971, it was also the first movie theater to open downtown since the Uptown Theatre opened in 1935. Movie theaters had been part of the trend of moving to the suburbs. But in 1970, the University of Missouri's admissions soared, hitting 21,687—up from 12,949 in 1961—and this meant there were plenty of moviegoers downtown again.

Initially, the Campus Twin was operated by the Mid-America Theatres chain. In 1985, Commonwealth Theaters was operating it, according to the 1985 Columbia City Directory.

By 1994, the Crown Cinema Corporation owned it along with Columbia's Mall 4 Theater and the Cinema Theatre. The Kansas City–based chain included 166 screens in Missouri, Kansas and Ohio.[136]

That year, the Campus Twin also changed the kinds of films it showed from first-run movies to a mix of foreign, specialized art films and independently made movies, the movies that wouldn't typically be shown at Columbia's

The Campus Twin, also known as the Campus Cinema I & II, opened in 1971 and closed in 1997. *Courtesy of Jeff Westbrook.*

mainstream or general interest theaters. For example, it showed *Eat Drink Man Woman*, which was acclaimed but not a top box office draw.[137]

The change was the Twin's response to the 1992 opening of the Forum 8.

But in 1997, Hollywood Theatres hit town and bought the Crown Cinema's holdings, including the Twin, the Cinema and the Mall 4. North America's fifteenth-largest movie chain with 475 screens at 77 locations, Hollywood opened its 14-screen complex the Hollywood Stadium 14 in September 1997 and closed the Campus Twin in November. In 1998, Hollywood closed the Cinema, and in 2000, it closed the Mall 4.

## MORE THAN MOVIES

For Jeff Westbrook, the Campus Twin is more than a historic footnote.

It's where he got his first job in 1973 at fifteen years old—making popcorn—made friends and even met his wife, Cherri. In a 2019 interview, he said he still misses working at the theaters. "The work gets in your blood." Ironically, he still works in a movie theater, but it, too, is closed. After a career in law enforcement, he works security at the Columbia Insurance Group, a company housed in the former White Gate Twin at 2102 Whitegate.

Westbrook started at the Campus Twin when he was fifteen and worked there for six years, during high school and while he attended the University of Missouri, majoring in psychology. For a high school project, he photographed the Twin, naming his photographic essay "The Theatre Never Sleeps."

At that time, the Twin's main crowd was college students, and the workforce was mostly high school and college students. The crew became a close, family-like group, he said.

"Some of us are still friends today," Westbrook added. He and his fellow workers took float trips together, played cards and watched movies. The Columbia movie theaters had reciprocal agreements, so if you worked at one theater, you could go to any movie theater for free, one of his favorite parts of the job.

But it wasn't all fun and games. Westbrook eventually became a projectionist, and that was challenging. The projectionist had to operate the projectors for both movies, the movie had to be framed correctly on the screen and the movies came in twenty-minute reels, which meant for an hour-long movie, the film had to be spliced together at three spots. Sometimes, he said, the splice didn't hold and the film would end up unreeling into a pile on the floor. "It was horrible. The crowd would be clapping, stomping, and your manager is up there," he said. "It didn't happen often, but it did happen a time or two. You had to stay on your toes."

Then, the small size of the Twin, the smallest in Columbia, with 298 seats in one auditorium and 291 in the other, meant that the ticket seller had to keep count so the theater wasn't oversold. It also meant the Twin never showed the biggest blockbusters such as *Jaws*, said Westbrook. It did, however, show some big productions such as *The Sting* and *Blazing Saddles*, the opening shows the night Westbrook began working there.

But for Westbrook, the draw wasn't just the movies. It was the friendship and atmosphere of the theater. "The best thing was the close-knit group," he said. Theaters are always more than the movies.

# 22

# BISCAYNE 3 CINEMAS, 1972–1998

## FROM FAMILY THEATER TO DOLLAR MOVIES

From its 1972 opening until its 1998 closing, the Biscayne 3 struggled to find its place—and even its name—in Columbia's crowded theater field. Ads in the November 23, 1972 *Columbia Missourian* said the Jerry Lewis Triple Cinema would be opening soon, and it promised family fare films and, the ad said, "Entertainment in a whole new world of comfort and luxury!"

By April 27, 1973, in an ad in the *Columbia Missourian*, the name had changed slightly to the Jerry Lewis Cinemas and featured a graphic of a bikini-clad woman. The movies being offered were *Three in the Cellar* and *Three in the Attic*, a 1968 film about swinging 1960s girls.

Frankly, it faced a lot of competition. At the time, Columbia had six operating movie theaters, including one drive-in. On May 1, 1973, it was renamed as the Biscayne III Theatre, according to Cinematreasures.org, but the confusion about its name didn't end. Newspaper ads in 1974 called it the Biscayne III Cinemas.

It also faced the challenge of opening in a shopping area that hadn't established a steady flow of customers or traffic. The Biscayne Mall at North Stadium and West Worley Street opened in 1972, and along with the movie theater, its occupants included a Montgomery Ward department store, a Woolco discount store and a freestanding McDonald's restaurant.

Additionally, the Biscayne Mall had to compete against the aging 1965 Parkade Plaza, but that was across town on the Business Loop. Then, in 1985, the Columbia Mall opened just a half mile away, and in February

1986, the Columbia 4 Mall Theatres opened. The Biscayne 3 began its downward spiral.

Then in 1992, the Dickinson opened the Forum 8 movie theaters and made the Biscayne a "cut-rate movie house" with one-dollar tickets.[138]

In 1997, the Hollywood Stadium 14, now the Regal Columbia & RPX, opened, but it was six miles away.

The final nail in the coffin struck on August 28, 1998, when the Hollywood chain, which also owned the Columbia 4 Mall Theatres, cut the mall theaters' ticket prices to a dollar.

For the Biscayne, that was it.

"On Monday, the Biscayne 3 grossed $44. The next day, Mission, Kansas-based Dickinson informed mall owner The Kroenke Group that it would vacate the theater by the end of October."[139]

A few years later, the Biscayne Mall was demolished, and today that space is occupied by the Shoppes at Stadium. The Biscayne 3 has faded into memory.

# 23

# WHITE/GATE VILLAGE TWIN THEATRE, 1973–1976

## A THREE-YEAR MYSTERY

Columbia's third multiplex lasted three years but never found its own niche.

Opened on July 27, 1973, as the White/Gate Cinema, its first ads in the *Columbia Daily Tribune* promised, "A new theatre of distinction."

By April 12, 1974, in an ad in the *Columbia Missourian*, its name had evolved to White Gate Village Twin Theatres.

The theater at 2102 Whitegate Drive closed in 1976, and as of this writing, the address is occupied by the Columbia Insurance Group. A drive to the address, along with some imagination, will let you see the former entrance to the two-screen suburban theater in the present office building.

The theater opened showing a mix of comedy and family fare and stuck with that formula. Opening night featured *Oklahoma Crude* at one screen and *Charlotte's Web* at the other.

Each auditorium seated 250 apiece, according to cinematreasures.org, and the theater eventually changed its name to the Twin. Perhaps the White Gate management was hoping to cash in on the move to the suburbs or the growth in Columbia north of I-70, but the competition of Columbia's seven other theaters proved too much and it closed in 1976.

In contrast to the Biscayne 3 Cinemas, which started as family-focused and quickly switched to offering whatever movies could bring in a crowd, the White Gate stuck with family movies. For example, *The Bad News Bears* screened there as part of its national preview starting on April 8, 1976, and ran for seven weeks, according to the website Digital Bits, which has been operating since 1997. The site says the White Gate was owned by Wehrenberg.

The White Gate does have a claim to fame: Open for only three years, it was Columbia's shortest-lived theater since 1909, when the Gem, Elite and Negro Nickelodeon operated briefly.

# COLUMBIA MALL 4 THEATRE, 1986–2000

## COLUMBIA'S LAST SHOPPING CENTER MULTIPLEX

Timing is everything, and in the case of the Columbia 4 Mall Theatres, it wasn't good.

Columbia's last shopping center movie theater and largest multiplex at that time opened in February 1986, just as video rentals of movies were challenging the movie theater industry. Recall that the nation's first Blockbuster retail video store opened just a year earlier.

The mall theaters closed in 2000 after fourteen years of movies and popcorn. Ironically, Barnes & Noble took over that space—and sells movies on DVDs as well as books and other items.

But in 1985, when the multiplex was under construction, a Commonwealth spokesman painted a rosy picture of the effect of the new technology on the movie industry and said, "Instead of creating costly competition for movies, video recorders, cable television and pay television services have actually extended the lives of many films." He added the entire theater industry was in an expansion phase, and Commonwealth planned on adding 140 screens over the next three years. At the time, Commonwealth was already the nation's sixth-largest chain. The representative also said movie admissions were increasing.[140]

History proved him wrong.

Movie admissions have never risen about the 1966 rate of 10 percent. In 1987, there were 22,679 screens, including drive-ins. In 2010, the numbers fell to 5,773.

Then, in May 1986, Commonwealth was sold to Cannon Group Inc., which picked up Commonwealth's $40 million to $50 million in debt as well as its 425 screens in the Midwest.[141]

## A NEW IDEA

Food courts must have been a novelty in the late 1980s, because an article published while the theater was under construction notes it would be next to the food court and then describes what a food court is in detail, stating it is "a dining area surrounded by a variety of fast-food restaurants." As for the theater itself, the article noted the lobby would be 16,000 square feet and the 1,100-seat-complex would feature 70mm film and Dolby stereo sound.[142]

When it opened, it featured projectors that could run continuously without needing to change reels or switch projectors, and one projectionist would run all four movie screen projectors. The theater opened with 1,000 seats in four auditoriums. A VIP event was held on February 28, with Mayor Rodney Smith, University of Missouri vice chancellor Duane Stucky and State Representatives Ken Jacob and Chris Kelly on hand as well as Commonwealth officials.[143]

Gone were the gala events that accompanied the openings of the Missouri Theatre or even the high school bands that accompanied the opening of the Uptown Theatre. Even the Cinema Theatre's 1966 opening night had featured the governor, but by 1986, local luminaries were the only celebrities on hand to welcome the four-screen theater.

The new multiplex wasn't all good news. After it opened, Commonwealth closed the Uptown, the Sky-Hi Drive-In and the Missouri Theatre. And the competition of videos? "The movies are the place to get away from home," said Commonwealth city manager David Jones. "This is the first place people go when they're out on their first date….The movies have a place in society and will remain."[144]

So far, he's right, and movie theaters still exist, but the Columbia Mall 4 closed on August 31, 2000, and the last four movies to be shown were *Gladiator*, *Me, Myself & Irene*, *Frequency* and *Big Momma's House*.

It didn't close because of movies on video but a bigger multiplex. Hollywood Theaters purchased the Mall 4 in 1997 and that year opened a fourteen-screen multiplex named the Hollywood Stadium 14, which is now the Regal Columbia & RPX. In August 1998, Hollywood turned the Mall 4 into a dollar movie house[145] and closed it two years later.

# HOLLYWOOD STADIUM 14/REGAL COLUMBIA AND RPX, 1997–PRESENT

## COLUMBIA'S LARGEST MULTIPLEX

O pened with fourteen screens in 1997, the Regal Columbia & RPX opened as the Hollywood Stadium 14 as Columbia's largest movie multiplex.

Its 2,752-seat capacity makes it Columbia's largest theater ever, topping the 2,000 seats of the 1902 Airdome.

But the Regal spent much of the 2020–21 coronavirus pandemic closed. It reopened on May 14, 2021. During the coronavirus pandemic, Columbia's public health order closed theaters on March 16, 2020. The Hollywood reopened briefly at some point but closed again in October 2020. In total, it was closed for twelve months between March 2020 and May 2021. Ironically, Columbia's two remaining small theaters, the Forum 8 and the Ragtag, spent less time closed during the pandemic.

In 1997, the Hollywood opened in a glory of bright lights, complete with a game area, meeting rooms and the luxurious seats moviegoers have come to expect. Located off the eastern end of Stadium at 2800 Goodwin Point, it offers acres of parking. At the time, it was owned by Hollywood Theatres, the fifteenth-largest exhibition chain in the United States.

Its opening heralded the doom of four movie theaters. Hollywood Theatres bought the holdings of Crown Cinema in Columbia, including the Campus Twin, the Cinema Theatre and the Columbia Mall 4. Hollywood promptly closed the Campus Twin, Columbia's first multiplex. The next year, it closed the Cinema Theatre, Columbia's last single-screen movie house. In 1998, it made the Columbia Mall 4 a dollar movie house,

Opened in 1997 as the Hollywood Stadium 14, it is operated now as the Regal Columbia & RPX, despite the remaining signs. *Courtesy of Deanna Dikeman, May 2021.*

driving the 1972 Biscayne 3 Cinemas owned by Dickinson out of business. Then, in 2000, Hollywood closed the Columbia Mall 4 Theatres.

In 2013, an even bigger chain came along and gobbled up the Hollywood. Regal Entertainment, the nation's largest exhibition chain, bought the Hollywood chain for roughly $191 million and the assumption of its $47 million in lease obligations.[146]

At the time, a newspaper article quoted a Regal spokesman as saying no changes were planned, "not even the Hollywood logo and branding on the theater at Stadium Boulevard and Highway 63."[147]

On December 5, 2017, Regal Entertainment was sold to UK–based Cineworld Group for $3.6 billion.[148] In October 2020, Cineworld closed five hundred Regal locations in the United States as well as theaters in the UK due to several major studios canceling releases of blockbuster films.[149]

In the twenty-four years it has been open, the former Hollywood Stadium 14 has seen the flood of video rental stores open and the last one close. It's endured the opening of the two-screen Ragtag Cinema, a niche market upstart. It's also endured the growth of streaming services from the start of Netflix to a mainstream habit for viewers.

Yet, as movie theater owners have known for decades, there's something magical about going to the movies, enjoying the refreshments and watching a flickering screen together. And so for the Regal, it began again on May 14, 2021.

# RAGTAG CINEMA, 1998-PRESENT

## FULL CIRCLE WITH A TWIST

The Ragtag Cinema brings Columbia's movie theater history full circle—but with a twist.

Instead of going for blockbusters and crowds, Ragtag Cinema has always specialized in niche, value-added or specialty movies and emphasized cooperation and community rather than an entrepreneurial approach.

The Ragtag is the only movie theater in Columbia's history operated by a nonprofit. Ragtag is run by the Ragtag Film Society, a nonprofit that runs both the cinema and True/False Film Fest.

As a movie theater, it can seem unique among Columbia's movie theaters—a microtheater in a reclaimed Coca-Cola bottling plant.

But is it unique? Yes and no.

Instead, it could be said the Ragtag Cinema encapsulates Columbia's entire movie theater history.

For starters, the Ragtag opened in 2000 at 23 North Tenth Street in an old storefront, replicating the start of one of Columbia's oldest movie theaters, the Nickelodeon, which opened in 1904 in a former hat shop and post office. Again, like many of the early movie theaters, the Ragtag changed its name. In 2008, the Ragtag Cinema changed its name from the Ragtag Cinemacafe.

Like many of the early movie theaters, Ragtag opened with scruffy seating, but instead of the benches early movie theaters used, the Ragtag's first location had seats, even if they were tattered couches and recycled office chairs. Its current location at 10 Hitt Street, where it moved in 2008, still

Ragtag Cinema moved to 10 Hitt Street in 2008 from its 23 North Tenth Street location. *Courtesy of Deanna Dikeman, May 2021.*

offers nontraditional movie seating, with 75 seats in one auditorium and 130 spots in the "big" theater made up of couches and easy chairs.

Yet, these two small spaces contrast sharply with the size of all of Columbia's movie theaters. Even Columbia's smallest early movie theater, the Nickel, had seating for 250.

The most important history the Ragtag replicates is the feeling of Columbia's early drive-in movie theaters and its movie palaces—that feeling of sharing the experience and a sense of community that makes movies matter.

## MOVIES + COMMUNITY = RAGTAG AND TRUE/FALSE

Yet, the Ragtag also is about more than the movies—just as it was for the early drive-in movie theaters and movie palaces.

The idea of a community coming together to see a movie is baked into both movie theater and the festival, said David Wilson, one of the founders of the Ragtag Film Society and the 2021 interim artistic director of True/False Film Fest. The international film fest was founded in 2004 and now draws thousands of people to Columbia each year. In 2020, roughly fourteen thousand people attended and thirty-seven thousand tickets were sold.

The 2020 fest concluded just as the coronavirus pandemic hit. Continuing virus concerns led to scheduling the 2021 Fest outside at Stephens Park from May 5–8, 2021, with films screened on five different screens. The 2021 event's draw fell to 9,500, made up of 7,450 in-person tickets and 2,050 online.[150]

All the movies shown at the Ragtag—not just those shown at the festival—are chosen and represent a "curated lineup," said Wilson. "It's intentional programming." While there are tens of thousands of movies made every year and streaming can seem like the offerings are endless, the major streaming venues offer only about three thousand. But how do you find movies worth your time? How do you make a movie more than something you can do from the comfort of your couch?

The answer is people trust Ragtag to screen the unusual, the unique, movies that will stick with you long after you leave the theater. But Wilson doesn't want those movies to feel like you're taking your vitamins—instead Ragtag is devoted to making a movie an event you're invited and welcomed to.

At the Ragtag, it means a movie might include anything from a concert or some kind of music, a lecture, a dialogue, a roundtable discussion—something beyond seeing the movie

As Paul Sturtz, the other founder of Ragtag, explained, both the movie theater and True/False are based on the idea that people want to gather in a welcoming spot with their neighbors and share a great movie.

And like those joyous days of the early drive-ins, going to Ragtag is also about the refreshments. Uprise Bakery, located in the same building as Ragtag, offers sandwiches, bakery items, a glass of wine or a good beer. As Wilson noted, quoting the German playwright Bertolt Brecht, "A theater without beer is just a museum."

## TIMING IS EVERYTHING

When the two founders met, Wilson, a Columbia native, had landed back in Columbia after graduating from Hampshire College in Massachusetts and was working at Leo's, a vintage clothing store. In 1995, Sturtz arrived in town from Portland following his 1989 graduation from the University of Oregon with a journalism degree and was working at the Missouri Rural Crisis Center, a family farm organization. Sturtz would later work at the *Columbia Daily Tribune* from 1998 to 1999, first as a reporter and then an editor.

The two met at a concert at the old Shattered nightclub in 1997 and hit it off; talk quickly turned to starting some kind of film series.

David Wilson and Paul Sturtz founded the Ragtag Film Society, which operates the Ragtag Cinema and the True/False Film Fest. *Courtesy of Olivia O Wyatt.*

The next day, Sturtz spoke to King, then owner of The Blue Note, and got an immediate nod to use the former movie theater to show films. King said Wilson and Sturtz reminded him of himself and his partner during their early days starting out. King gave Wilson and Sturtz what he called "a crazy cheap rate" for using the live music venue on Sunday and Wednesday nights, figuring the movies would end before The Blue Note's crowd arrived.

At about the same time, mainstream movie theaters were closing, creating a space for Ragtag. In 1997, the downtown Campus Twin, which had been showing art house movies, closed. In 1998, both the Cinema Theatre in the Broadway Shopping Center and Columbia's cheap movie house, the Biscayne 3 Cinemas, closed.

On January 18, 1998, Wilson and Sturtz and a group of volunteers kicked off a movie series that started with the *Year of the Horse*, a concert documentary with Neil Young. They continued with several seasons of series, at first making only enough to buy a popcorn maker and then a 16mm movie projector to replace the projector they'd borrowed.

In 2000, the two were approached by Holly Roberson, Tim Spence and Ron Rottinghaus with the idea of opening up a bakery, café and movie theater. "Paul and I were content doing the series," said Wilson, but the chemistry was right and the group moved ahead.

The new entrepreneurs called their business venture Bonavita Enterprises, and in June 2000, they teamed up with Wilson and Sturtz and showed *Waiting for Guffman* in a former storefront they turned into a tiny theater at 23 North Tenth Street. They called the new theater the Ragtag Cinemacafe. It boasted enough room for seventy seats, with couches and ratty chairs and a tiny bar, but it wasn't big enough for the bakery the five had envisioned. So for a while, Uprise was housed at 816 East Broadway.

Again, timing helped. In 2000, the Columbia Mall 4 closed, leaving only four operating movie theaters: the Forum 8, the Hollywood 14 and Ragtag and the adult Olde Un Theatres.

In 2004, Ragtag Cinemacafe became a nonprofit named Ragtag Programming for Film and Media Art, later the Ragtag Film Society.

In 2008, Ragtag moved to its current home, 10 Hitt Street, uniting the Ragtag Cinema, Uprise Bakery and 9th Street Video, which closed in 2016. The move followed fundraising efforts that involved Ragtag collecting $250,000 for screens, curtains, seating and other items to furnish its new space.

## ECONOMIC ENGINE

Early movie theaters were huge moneymakers. Recall in 1909, a newspaper noted movie theaters saw a greater flow of cash than the banks. That kind of cashflow led to entrepreneurs building three movie palaces in Columbia from 1916 to 1928 and three other smaller movie theaters opening from 1935 to 1949.

But Ragtag Cinema has never been flush with funds. As noted, the Ragtag Cinema is a nonprofit that does significant fundraising to keep it and the True/False Film Fest going.

But it has moved beyond the early years. Sturtz said it was 2007 or 2008 before the festival began paying "real" salaries, but "we were scrappy," getting by on the minimum. Sturtz said for years he lived in a 370-square-foot granny flat in the Benton-Stephens area for a few hundred dollars a month so he could live on a minimal salary.

Wilson echoed his sentiment and recalled back when they literally made the theater's tickets by photocopying them and cutting them into individual tickets.

Today, Ragtag and True/False has grown beyond those ragged years. In 2021, Ragtag employed twelve people, and True/False had a $2 million budget. It is now led by three executives: Barbie Banks, Camellia Cosgray and Arin Liberman.

Both organizations have grown in another way as well.

In 2018, Wilson stepped down from programming, only stepping back recently as an interim for the 2021 True/False Fest. In 2019, Sturtz left Ragtag and True/False to get involved in Elizabeth Warren's bid for president. In February 2021, he became codirector of nonprofit Upstate Films, which operates two movie houses in the Hudson Valley.

But True/False Film Fest does generate money. It is a documented economic engine for Columbia. A 2018 Economic Impact Study estimated True/False's economic impact at roughly $2.2 million spent in Columbia for lodging, meals, transportation, shopping, entertainment and tickets.[151]

But despite streaming and the pandemic that closed the Ragtag for periods of time in 2020, both Sturtz and Wilson see a future ahead for the theater and the festival.

"I'm convinced that art house destinations with community-oriented events will survive," said Sturtz. "It's human nature to want to get out of the house and be a part of a community."

History is on his side.

# NOTES

## Chapter 1

1. Alan R. Havig, *From Southern Village to Midwestern City* (Woodland Hills, CA: Windsor Publications, 1984), 26.
2. Scott Bomboy, "The Day the Supreme Court Killed Hollywood's Studio System," Constitution Daily, May 24, 2021, https://constitutioncenter.org/blog/the-day-the-supreme-court-killed-hollywoods-studio-system/.

## Chapter 2

3. "Haden Opera House Burns—Buildings Damaged—Loss $60,000," *Columbia Missouri Herald*, March 1, 1901, 1.
4. Brennan David, "Once a Sought-out Eatery, Haden House Riddled with Crime," *Columbia Daily Tribune*, November 20, 2011, https://www.columbiatribune.com/article/20111120/News/311209850.
5. "Haden's Opera House," *Weekly Missouri Statesman*, January 25, 1884.
6. "Big Blaze at Columbia," *Henry County Democrat*, March 3, 1901.
7. *Columbia Missouri Statesman*, May 28, 1897.
8. Joe E. Smith, "Early Movies and Their Impact on Columbia," *Missouri Historical Review*, 74, no. 7 (October 1979): 73.

## Chapter 3

9. "Columbia's First Theatre Was in Abandoned Church House," *Columbia Evening Missourian*, June 14, 1922.
10. "Hippodrome Totally Destroyed Tuesday," *Evening Missourian*, February 19, 1919.
11. "New Site for the Airdome," *University Missourian*, March 12, 1909.
12. Advertisement, *University Missourian*, October 14, 1915.
13. "Don't Ask For It: Get It Yourself," *University Missourian*, November 12, 1914.
14. "The Girls Must Quit Kissing His Patrons," *University Missourian*, February 17, 1916.
15. "He Won't Cater to the Masses," *University Missourian*, April 27, 1916.

## Chapter 4

16. Mary J. Matthews, Office of Historic Preservation Historic Inventory, May 9, 1979, revised November 19, 1979, https://dnr.mo.gov/shpo/survey/BOAS002-S.pdf.
17. Smith, "Early Movies," 75.
18. Ibid.
19. "Nickelodeons Have 'First Nighters,'" *University Missourian*, October 8, 1908.
20. "Making Odeons Safe from Fire," *University Missourian*, February 16, 1909.
21. "The Moving Picture Craze," *University Missourian*, November 1, 1911.
22. "3,500 Attend Picture Shows Here Daily," *University Missourian*, February 12, 1911.
23. "Direct Talks," *University Missourian*, February 25, 1912.
24. "Two Theaters Combined," *University Missourian*, January 24, 1916.
25. "Theaters Combine," *Evening Missourian*, January 18, 1918.
26. "Oldest Picture House Sold," *Evening Missourian*, April 4, 1919.
27. "'Birth of a Nation' Coming," *Evening Missourian*, May 17, 1919.

## Chapter 5

28. "Horsehair Couch, Signboard All that Remain of Theater," *Columbia Daily Tribune*, July 31, 1951.

29. "Columbia Was Always a 'Show Town,'" *Columbia Missourian Progress Edition*, February 1953.

30. "Columbia Theatre Damaged by Fire," *Moberly Monitor-Index*, March 4, 1929.

31. "'100 Years Later: What's the Legacy of '*Birth of a Nation*,'" NPR, *All Things Considered*, February 8, 2015, https://www.npr.org/sections/cod eswitch/2015/02/08/383279630/100-years-later-whats-the-legacy-of-birth-of-a-nation.

32. "Action Taken by Local Pastors of Local Churches after a Mass Meeting," *University Missourian*, May 22, 1916.

## Chapter 6

33. An ad for the Gem, *University Missourian*, March 12, 1909.

34. "Nickel Movies Do Big Business," *University Missourian*, November 17, 1909.

35. Ibid.

36. "Negros Don't Like Nickel Theaters," *University Missourian*, May 17, 1910.

37. No headline, text ad for a moving picture exhibit, *The Professional World*, October 31, 1902.

38. "The Negro in Columbia," *University Missourian*, March 29, 1911.

39. "Fire in Fifth Street Home," *University Missourian*, April 29, 1909.

40. Text notice, *University Missourian*, September 23, 1908.

41. Smith, "Early Movies," 75.

## Chapter 7

42. "Tom Thumb Wedding," *University Missourian*, October 16, 1913.

43. "Two Theaters Combined," *University Missourian*, January 24, 1916.

44. "Another New Theater Here," *Evening Missourian*, June 2, 1919.

45. "Columbians Like Silent Drama," *University Missourian*, September 14, 1914.

46. Ibid.

47. Ibid.

## Chapter 8

48. "The Hall Theatre, Souvenir Section," *Daily Missourian*, August 27, 1916.
49. Ibid.
50. Ibid.
51. Ibid
52. "Group Sees New Life in Old Hall Theatre," *Columbia Missourian*, May 1, 1974.
53. "Hall Theater: Bygone Era May Be Resurrected," *Columbia Missourian*, July 19, 1985.
54. "New Minimall Opens Monday," *Columbia Daily Tribune*, June 25, 1993.
55. Kim Dickey, "Hall Theater Renovation Project in the Works," *Columbia Missourian*, September 27, 1991.
56. Theodore P. Roth, "St. Louis Bread Co. to Open in Hall Theater," *Columbia Daily Tribune*, October 2, 1993.
57. *Centralia Fireside Guard*, September 13, 1873.
58. "Columbia Theatre Company and T.C. Hall Own All Local Houses," *Columbia Daily Tribune*, September 15, 1926.
59. Maude Hall Jones, *The Philosophy of Thomas C. Hall* (Moberly, MO: Message Print, c. 1945).

## Chapter 9

60. "Rex Barrett Retires!" *Bright Side*, January 1961.
61. "Cozy Is To Be Remodeled," *Columbia Evening Missourian*, March 2, 1922.
62. "Pipe Organ Now Being Installed at the Cozy," *Columbia Evening Missourian*, November 17, 1922.
63. "Modern Methods Work Wonders in Columbia, Missouri, House," *Universal Weekly*, November 2, 1923.
64. "Cozy Theater to Open Sundays," *Columbia Daily Tribune*, July 11, 1925.
65. "Churches Disapprove Sunday Amusements," *Columbia Daily Tribune*, August 25, 1925.
66. "T.C. Hall Owns All Local Houses. CHANGE SEPT. 1," *Columbia Daily Tribune*, August 3, 1926.
67. "Oldest Theatre Will Be Closed," *Columbia Daily Tribune*, May 17, 1927.

## Chapter 10

68. "Varsity Theatre Opens Last Night," *Columbia Daily Tribune*, October 4, 1927.
69. "Varsity Design Is Latest Type," *Columbia Missourian*, October 6, 1927.
70. Ibid.
71. "Varsity Theatre to Open Tonight," *Columbia Daily Tribune*, October 3, 1927.
72. "Varsity Theater to Open Monday," *Columbia Daily Tribune*, September 26, 1927.
73. "Homer Woods Is Found Dead in His Office," *Columbia Missourian*, July 5, 1955.
74. "Homer G. Woods Found Dead in Theatre Office," *Columbia Daily Tribune*, July 5, 1955.
75. Ibid.
76. Ibid.
77. Ibid.
78. "Hall, Varsity Leased By Commonwealth Chain," *Columbia Daily Tribune*, June 29, 1955.
79. Mark Hirsch, "Varsity Slated for New Nightclub Act," *Columbia Daily Tribune*, July 1, 1988.
80. Mick Normington, "Comic Book Club Closes Its Doors," *Columbia Missourian*, February 22, 1989.

## Chapter 11

81. "Missouri Theatre Opening October 5," *Columbia Daily Tribune*, September 17, 1928.
82. Marie Sloan, *Missouri Theatre: Visions of the Past and the Future*, State Historical Society of Missouri, date uncertain, 2002 or 2003, pages unnumbered.
83. Ronda Corneliusm, "Missouri Theatre Considers Keeping Segregation's Relic," *Columbia Missourian*, March 23, 1995.
84. Taylor Wanbaugh, "The Missouri Theatre, a Columbia Tradition," *CoMo Mag*, April 2014.
85. "Columbia Theater Sold for $20,500," *University Missourian*, October 12, 1908.
86. Matthews, Historic Inventory, https://dnr.mo.gov/shpo/survey/BOAS002-S.pdf.

87. "New Theater Opens Tomorrow Evening," *Columbia Missourian*, October 4, 1928.
88. Ibid.
89. Noelle Soren, National Register of Historic Places Nomination Form: Missouri Theater, 203 South Ninth Street, Columbia, Missouri, January 4, 1979.
90. "New Theater Opens Tomorrow Evening," *Columbia Missourian*, October 4, 1928.
91. Sloan, *Missouri Theatre*.
92. "Profit in a Theater 'War,'" *Kansas City Times*, January 8, 1929.
93. "Churches Protest Sunday Theatres," *Columbia Daily Tribune*, October 7, 1929.

## Chapter 12

94. "Uptown Theater Opens Doors Tonight," *Columbia Missourian*, May 18, 1935.
95. "703 Soft Seats to Feature Comfort," *Columbia Missourian*, May 18, 1935.
96. "Girl Attaches of Uptown Theater," *Columbia Missourian*, May 18, 1935.
97. "Simplicity Marks All Decorations," *Columbia Missourian*, May 18, 1935.
98. "Even Temperatures To Be Maintained," *Columbia Missourian*, May 18, 1935.
99. Mary Beth Brown, "The Struggle in the Show-Me State," *Missouri Life*, January/February 2021, https://missourilife.com/the-struggle-in-the-show-me-state/.
100. "CORE Group of 30 Protests Theater's Racial Segregation," *Columbia Daily Tribune*, November 17, 1953.
101. Ibid.

## Chapter 14

102. Ad for the Frances, *Columbia Daily Tribune*, February 18, 1949.
103. "Columbia Was Always a 'Show Town,'" *Columbia Missourian Progress Edition*, February 1953.
104. Princess Pam ad, *Columbia Missourian*, February 15, 1959.
105. "Sharp End: The 1930s," *Columbia Daily Tribune*, May 20, 2015.
106. "A Fresh Memory of Sharp End," *CoMo Mag*, August 26, 2016.

107. "DEATH: Edward 'Dick' Tibbs," *Columbia Missourian*, April 22, 1986.
108. "Sharp End: The 1930s," *Columbia Daily Tribune*, May 20, 2015.

## Chapter 15

109. Ad for Broadway Drive-In Theatre, *Columbia Daily Tribune*, June 11, 1949.
110. "530-car Drive-In Theater Will Be Built at Columbia," *Moberly (MO) Monitor-Index*, February 18, 1949.
111. Kerry Segrave, *Drive-In Theaters: A History from their Inception in 1933* (Jefferson, NC: McFarland & Company, 1992), 89.
112. Ibid., 65.

## Chapter 16

113. Thomas W. Parry Jr., "A Home in Booth Building Is Unique," *Box Office Magazine*, July 1953.
114. Ibid.
115. Ibid.
116. "Former City Mayor Herb Jeans Dies," *Columbia Daily Tribune*, March 9, 1975.
117. Ibid.
118. "Herbert Jeans, Ex-Mayor, Businessman, Dies at 63," *Columbia Missourian*, March 9, 1975.
119. "Former City Mayor Herb Jeans Dies," *Columbia Daily Tribune*, March 9, 1975.
120. Ad, *Columbia Daily Tribune*, March 27, 1953.
121. Ad, *Columbia Missourian*, March 6, 1959.

## Chapter 17

122. "Sky-Hi Drive-In Opens Wednesday Night," *Columbia Missourian*, June 27, 1965.
123. Sky-Hi Drive-In Opens," *Columbia Missourian*, February 18, 1966.
124. "Sky-Hi Drive-In Opens Wednesday Night."
125. Ad, *Columbia Missourian*, April 27, 1973.

## Chapter 18

126. "Hollywood Closes Cinema Theater," *Columbia Daily Tribune*, November 30, 1998.
127. Ad, *Columbia Missourian*, June 6, 1966.
128. Ibid.
129. "Cinema Theater to Open with Glass Bottom Boat," *Columbia Missourian*, June 7, 1966.
130. "Commonwealth Plans Big Columbia House," *Boxoffice*, February 1, 1965.
131. "Cinema Theater to Open with Glass Bottom Boat."
132. Ibid.

## Chapter 19

133. Grant Miller, "Columbia's Movie Theaters Continue to Thwart COVID-19 for Now," *Vox*, March 2021.
134. Travis Clark, "How the Movie-Theater Industry Will Be Permanently Changed by the Pandemic, as Major Hollywood Studios Rethink Their Release Strategies," *Business Insider*, March 30, 2021, https://www.businessinsider.com/how-major-hollywood-movie-studios-are-collapsing-the-theatrical-window-2021-3?op=1.
135. "Forum 8, Capital 8 Theaters Reopen," *Columbia Daily Tribune*, September 2, 2020.

## Chapter 21

136. Theodore P. Roth, "Campus Twin Offers Specialized, Art Films," *Columbia Daily Tribune*, October 4, 1994.
137. Ibid.

## Chapter 22

138. "Dickinson Set to Launch Dollar Theater," *Columbia Daily Tribune*, July 29, 1992.
139. Paul Sturtz, "Biscayne 3 to Show Its Last Reel—Trend Toward Luxurious Multiplex Theaters Plays a Role," *Columbia Daily Tribune*, September 4, 1998.

## Chapter 24

140. Dolores Whiskeyman, "Theater Complex Set for Mall," *Columbia Daily Tribune*, March 2, 1985.
141. Geraldine Fabrikant, "Cannon to Buy Chain of Theaters," *New York Times*, May 8, 1986.
142. Whiskeyman, "Theater Complex Set for Mall."
143. Chris Ganschow and Gloria Nobleza, "Theater Complex Opening Tonight at Columbia Mall," *Columbia Missourian*, February 28, 1986.
144. Whiskeyman, "Theater Complex Set for Mall."
145. Sturtz, "Biscayne 3 to Show Its Last Reel."

## Chapter 25

146. Georg Szalai, "Regal Entertainment to Acquire Hollywood Theaters in $238 Million Deal," *Hollywood Reporter*, February 19, 2013.
147. Jacob Barker, "Hollywood Stadium 14 Theater Facing No Changes in New Hands," *Columbia Daily Tribune*, June 15, 2013.
148. Nathan Bomey, "Regal Movie Theater Chain Being Sold as More Film Fans Stay Home," *USA Today*, December 5, 2017.
149. Douglas Jones, "Regal Cinemas Temporarily Closing All of Its US Theaters," AP News report, October 4, 2020.

## Chapter 26

150. Ciara McCaskill, "Spirits High Despite Lower Numbers amid COVID-Related Adjustments for True/False 2021," *Columbia Missourian*, May 21, 2021.
151. Kim Dae-Young, Yejin Lee and Seunghwan Lee, "Final Survey Report: Economic Impact Study, True and False Film Festival," *University of Missouri, Hospitality Management*, June 2018.

# INDEX

# ABOUT THE AUTHOR

Dianna Borsi O'Brien isn't a native of Columbia, but she wishes she was! She came to Columbia in 1991 to attend the School of Journalism at the University of Missouri and fell in love with the city. After moving away for several years to work in the newspaper business, Dianna came back to Columbia and took up freelancing. Then, in 2010, a magazine assignment to write about the city's historic properties program led to her falling in love with learning and writing about Columbia history, a love that hasn't abated since.

That love ushered her into creating a website to share her enthusiasm about Columbia's amazing history from movie theaters to cemeteries and everything in between. That site, CoMoHistoricPlaces.com, continues to grow and draws hundreds of visitors every month.

In 2019, the city started planning to celebrate its bicentennial in 2021, and a friend on the planning taskforce asked Dianna to create a timeline of Columbia's movie theaters. The result was a book digging up forgotten movie houses and the names and dates of the men—and women—behind the city's movie theaters.

When she's not looking for some obscure historic detail for her website, Dianna can be found reading, hiking or traveling with her husband or walking her naughty dog, Zippy.

Today, she calls herself an accidental historian and continues to share her finds on CoMoHistoricPlaces.com

*Visit us at*
www.historypress.com